THE DOLCE DIET

LIVING LEAN
COOKBOOK

by MIKE DOLCE
with BRANDY ROON

Conrad James Books
Las Vegas, NV

conradjamesbooks.com

Printed in the United States of America.

ISBN 978-0-9849631-2-6

Edited by Brandy Roon
Cover Design by Zack Sherman
Interior layout Design by Jun Hanawa

CONTENTS

BREAKFAST

LUNCH

DINNER

SIDES & SNACKS

SMOOTHIES

INTRODUCTION

Welcome to The Dolce Diet: LIVING LEAN Cookbook!

I can't believe the amazing success we've had with The Dolce Diet: LIVING LEAN, which became a Barnes & Noble #1 bestseller the first week of its release!

It was incredible, especially considering all of our products are self-published.

Why did we decide to self-publish our book? Simple. We wanted to stay true to form. We'd been approached by multiple publishing houses that all wanted to release their versions of The Dolce Diet.

Initially, it was very exciting. Brandy and myself were flown to meetings to discuss the possibilities of such a partnership. At that point, it was the epitome of our dreams to sign with a big publishing house, but through discussions we realized our ideas and theirs did not mesh.

They wanted to bastardize the true form of The Dolce Diet. They wanted to box it, to build walls and ceilings and boundaries around what we do. They wanted me to make it scientific, for me to profess how smart I was, how much more I knew than everybody else and, for those of you who know me, that's not me at all!

Yes, I am the most famous weight reduction expert in the sport of mixed martial arts.

Yes, I have more UFC Pay-Per-View main event athletes coming to me to direct their training camps, weight loss, nutrition strategies, strength-and-conditioning, and peaking and periodization programs than any other coach in this sport.

Yes, I have thousands of clients from around the world who've lost countless amounts of weight.

Yes, I myself lost 110 pounds in a short period of time.

So YES, I am the expert most of you already know.

This is why you have this book. I don't need to waste chapters, like many authors do, using 100 words to say what can and should be said in 10 words.

I'm not knocking any other system, although most are fads.

I'm not knocking other authors, although most are in it for greed.

All I do is let you know what works in the simplest form possible.

We have lives we want to live in the healthiest ways possible and we don't have time to spend 10 hours in our kitchens making one meal.

The Dolce Diet: LIVING LEAN is a simple concept that can be embraced by the neurosurgeon, the high school student, the prenatal mom, the high-powered attorney, the professional fighter and my 87-year-old grandmother.

That's the beauty of it. It's easy.

That's why The Dolce Diet: LIVING LEAN is a #1 international bestseller without the backing of a major publisher, and that's why this companion cookbook is here for you now.

The exponential growth of The Dolce Diet has been based solely on word of mouth.

A co-worker will lose weight and be asked, "How did you do it?"

A teammate will gain huge leaps in strength, conditioning and fat loss and be asked, "What did you change?" A family member will have energy not seen in years and be asked, "What are you doing differently?"

The answer is THE DOLCE DIET.

Why? Because it works.

In The Dolce Diet: LIVING LEAN we featured several amazing recipes. We gave you a complete meal plan and discussed how to implement those recipes. We gave you workouts, strength training, body toning and cardiovascular training routines - everything you need to build a healthy foundation and maintain a vibrant, active life.

We also gave you the reasons why it works. In LIVING LEAN, I share stories with you about my childhood and fill you in on exactly how my history formed my health approach of today.

As in LIVING LEAN, this cookbook does not waste time exploring the caloric breakdown of each crumb. If you want to know how many grams of carbohydrates there are in a slice of whole wheat bread, Google it.

The LIVING LEAN Cookbook is a continuation of the recipes in The Dolce Diet: LIVING LEAN book.

Though I still have the Breakfast Bowl almost every day, and I love my Egg Scrambles for lunch and my Salmon Salads are amazing, I'm blown away by the tastiness and ease of these new recipes.

There are Vegan, Gluten-Free, Athlete and Health-Minded options. These recipes will work for most everyone, often with just minor changes.

We've received hundreds of reviews and testimonials about LIVING LEAN and now we can't wait to hear what you think of these recipes!

Every day, I check my Twitter feed (@thedolcediet) to see thousands of testimonials from people around the world who love this program.

And, in case you were wondering, no, we do not have a marketing firm propelling The Dolce Diet brand forward. We have something way better.

YOU!

YOUR results!

Yes, actual folks from around the world who use The Dolce Diet principles to achieve their health goals!

There is no gimmick on the planet that can trump the truth.

So go explore this cookbook, experiment, tweak to your liking and your lifestyle, and try new things! Take pictures and post them to me on Twitter! I love to see what everyone is doing!

Remember, we're in this together. We can inspire each other and motivate each other, but we must always be accountable to ourselves.

Please share these recipes with your family and friends. Bring a dish to your office or a neighbor's birthday party. Help spread the joy of health, wellness and easy weight loss.

What would the world be like if your friends and family were all too sick, tired and lifeless to share the coming decades with you?

These recipes are inexpensive and easy to prepare. Of course, they are also highly nutritious and so delicious you'll wonder why you didn't start sooner. Pancakes, fried chicken, chili and burritos on a diet? That's right!

Here's to one positive step at a time!

— Mike Dolce

Praise for The Dolce Diet: LIVING LEAN

The Dolce Diet, three words about Living Lean: 1. Simple 2. Inspirational 3. Effective. Thank you, Mike Dolce! You've made staying in shape easy!
— *STEWART M.*

The Dolce Diet, Love it! My Little-Boy-2-B has been on it for 5.5 months! This diet is truly amazing for moms pre & post baby! Yes, The Dolce Diet is prego friendly! Plenty of the RIGHT kind of food that tastes great!
— *THE H2H WAITRESS*

Started two weeks ago. Lost 13 pounds so far. Yea! Love the recipes! So do my kids! Thank you!
— *DAWN H.*

Body fat down 4% in 2 months?! Yessss! #LIVING LEAN
— *MOLLY C.*

The Dolce Diet: Started 410, down 50 lbs. so far.
— *JOSH W.*

The Dolce Diet: 13 lbs. lost in 4 weeks! People are asking what I'm doing...Telling them LIVING LEAN!
— *MIKE S.*

Real talk! The Dolce Diet is the Einstein, da Vinci and Jesus of losing weight all wrapped up in one...gluten free wrap that is.
— *MIKEY F.*

Another 5 (lbs. lost) on The Dolce Diet. 25 pounds down in 2 weeks, 100 to go! #LivingLean!
— *JOHN P.*

Making THE DOLCE DIET turkey burgers. LIVING LEAN and loving it!
— *JULIE W.*

The Dolce Diet, I've lost 35 lbs. of fat since January 3rd. Healthy and delicious! I love Living Lean.
— *BRANDON E.*

I can't walk! That means I had a great booty workout!! Yeah buddy! #LIVINGLEAN
— *MARI C.*

The Dolce Diet, 31 lbs. lost now. Feeling great. Can't believe I didn't do this before. 16 lbs. to go.
— *JEFF S.*

24 lbs. in 6 weeks! BOOM! All thanks to The Dolce Diet & Living Lean!
— *CHRIS P.*

Day 40 tastes just as good! Mike Dolce is the Weight Whisperer.
— *STEPHANIE S.*

THE DOLCE DIET

LIVING LEAN
COOKBOOK

by MIKE DOLCE
with BRANDY ROON

RECIPE KEY

Note: These recipes are easily interchangeable with vegan, gluten-free, health-minded and athletic lifestyles. Experiment, tweak and enjoy!

Recipe Key

V = Vegan friendly (no animal products)

G= Gluten friendly

H = Health-minded

A = Athlete friendly

BREAKFAST

BLUEBERRY COCONUT BUCKWHEAT BOWL

(V, G, H, A) | SERVES 1

Ingredients

1/4 cup organic buckwheat

**1/3 cup unsweetened shredded coconut
(keep a palmful of coconut on the side for toasting)**

1 cup water

1/4 cup plain almond milk

sprinkle of Saigon cinnamon

1/3 cup blueberries (fresh or frozen)

1 Tbsp. agave (V) or honey

Directions

1. In a small pot, bring water to a boil and add buckwheat and coconut. Reduce heat and simmer.

2. After about 3 minutes, when buckwheat starts to thicken, add in blueberries, mix and cover. Mixture should thicken in about 4-5 minutes. Remove from heat, stir and cover.

3. In a small pan, toast the extra coconut flakes and set aside.

4. Back to the buckwheat: Drizzle in agave, cinnamon and almond milk (be careful not to make the mixture too thin). Buckwheat tends to keep thickening even after removed from heat.

5. Put in bowl and top with toasted coconut flakes. Enjoy!

EGGS, GREENS & BEAN BURRITO

(G, H, A) | SERVES 1

Ingredients

2 eggs

handful spinach

1/3 cup red or black beans

sprinkle of white, sharp cheddar (optional)

3 thin slices avocado (optional)

dash of pepper

Bragg All Natural Herb & Spice Seasoning (optional)

1 tsp. Vegenaise spread (optional)

1 whole wheat or gluten-free wrap

Directions

1. Scramble eggs, and then mix in beans and seasoning when eggs are almost done. Stir well.
2. Spread Vegenaise onto wrap.
3. Grate cheese onto wrap and add cooked eggs and beans.
4. Top with spinach and sliced avocado.
5. Wrap up tightly and enjoy!

GRANOLA BERRY SMASH

(G, H, A) | SERVES 1

Ingredients

- **1/4 cup blueberries**
- **1/4 cup strawberries**
- **1/4 cup granola**
- **splash of unsweetened almond milk**
- **dash of cinnamon**

Directions

1. Warm berries in small pot and put in bowl.
2. Top with granola and a splash of almond milk. Sprinkle with cinnamon.
3. Enjoy!

STEEL CUT OATS & DATES

(V, H, A) | SERVES 1-2

Ingredients

1/4 cup steel cut oats

3/4 cup water or almond milk

dash of cinnamon

1/4 cup chopped dates

Directions

1. Bring water to a boil.

2. Add oats, dates and dash of cinnamon and then simmer for about 20 minutes.

3. Remove from heat and let stand for 2-3 minutes before serving.

HARDBOILED EGGS & AVOCADO BREAKFAST SALAD

(G, H, A) | SERVES 1

Ingredients

2 hard-boiled eggs

1/2 avocado, peeled

sprinkle of pepper

sprinkle of sea salt

dash of paprika

1 tsp. Vegenaise (optional)

Directions

1. Peel eggs, and then add to small bowl and mash.
2. Add in avocado and mash with eggs.
3. Mix in Vegenaise, salt, pepper and paprika.
4. Mix well and enjoy!
5. This also goes great on your favorite healthy bread or wrap!

TATER TOTS

(V, G, H, A) | SERVES 4-6

Note: Serve these breakfast potatoes with your favorite egg recipe.

Ingredients

8 red potatoes, cut into bite-sized pieces

1/4 bell pepper, diced

1/2 onion, chopped

2 cloves garlic, chopped

2 Tbsp. grapeseed oil

Sea salt, to taste

Black pepper, to taste

Directions

1. In large pan, heat grapeseed oil on medium and add potatoes, mixing frequently.

2. When potatoes begin to brown, add in onion, bell pepper and garlic and continue mixing about another 10 minutes until potatoes are tender.

3. Sprinkle with salt and pepper.

4. Serve hot.

OMELET
(G, H, A) | SERVES 1

Ingredients

3 whole eggs

1/4 diced red pepper

1/4 diced onion

1/4 cup almond milk

1 cup mushrooms, sliced

handful spinach leaves

dash of sea salt

1 slice Havarti cheese (optional)

Directions

1. Lightly coat 2 medium sauté pans with grapeseed oil and put on low heat.

2. Dice peppers, onions and mushrooms. Add to pan #1. Sauté for about 2 minutes and add mushrooms.

3. Whip eggs and milk in medium mixing bowl.

4. Once the vegetables begin to soften, add spinach leaves to pan #1.

5. Once spinach has begun to wilt, remove pan #1 from heat.

6. Evenly pour eggs into pan #2 so they coat the bottom of the pan and cover. (Do not stir.)

7. Once eggs harden, flip the omelet over and immediately add contents of pan #1 and cheese slice to half of the omelet. Fold the empty omelet half over on top and serve.

EGG SCRAMBLE

(G, H, A) | Serves 1-2

Ingredients

3 whole eggs

1/4 diced red pepper

1/4 diced onion

1 cup mushrooms, sliced

handful spinach leaves

dash of sea salt

1 slice white cheese (optional)

Also:

1/3 avocado, smeared on toast

2 slices toasted bread

Directions

1. Lightly coat medium sauté pan with grapeseed oil and put on low heat.

2. Dice peppers and onions and add to pan. Sauté about 2 minutes, then add mushrooms.

3. Whip eggs in medium mixing bowl.

4. Once the peppers, onions and mushrooms soften, add spinach leaves.

5. Once spinach begins to wilt, evenly pour eggs into pan.

6. Lightly stir into a scramble.

7. Once desired consistency is reached, turn off stovetop, mix in cheese and serve with toast smeared with avocado.

TOFU & KALE SCRAMBLE

(V, G, H, A) | SERVES 2-4

Ingredients

1 green bell pepper, diced

8 oz. mushrooms, sliced

2 cloves garlic, minced

15 oz. of tofu, firm or extra-firm, crumbled

1 1/2 tsp. smoked paprika

1 tsp. ground cumin

sea salt, to taste

dash of turmeric

handful kale

1/4 cup nutritional yeast

Directions

1. Sauté mushrooms, pepper and garlic in grapeseed oil on medium heat until tender.
2. Add the tofu, stirring often. Add the spices followed by the kale.
3. Add a tsp. of water, cover and steam, stirring every minute or so, until the kale wilts.
4. Mix in the nutritional yeast and cook for 2 more minutes until hot throughout.
5. Serve and enjoy!

SPINACH, BELL PEPPER & MUSHROOM FRITATTA

(G, H, A) | SERVES 2-4

Ingredients

2 Tbsp. grapeseed oil

8 eggs

1/2 cup almond milk

2 garlic cloves, minced

2 cups baby spinach, chopped

1 sweet onion, chopped

1 green bell pepper, chopped

5 oz. crimini mushrooms

sea salt, to taste

black pepper, to taste

ketchup, for dipping (optional)

Directions

1. Heat large pan with grapeseed oil and add garlic, spinach, onion, mushrooms and green pepper.
2. Cook about 4 minutes or until vegetables are tender.
3. In a small bowl, mix eggs and milk and add to vegetable pan, reduce heat to a simmer and cover.
4. Cook about 8 minutes.
5. Cut into wedges and serve.

COCONUT FRUIT CUPS

(V, G, H, A) | SERVES 2

Ingredients

- **1 mango, chopped**
- **1 peach, chopped**
- **2 kiwis, peeled & chopped**
- **1/2 lb. grapes**
- **1/4 cup pecans, crushed**
- **1/2 cup grated unsweetened coconut**
- **1/4 cup fresh squeezed orange juice**

Directions

1. Combine ingredients and mix well.
2. Put into small serving bowls.
3. Refrigerate for 1 hour.
4. Serve.

PITBULL PANCAKES

(V, G, H, A)　|　SERVES 4-6

Ingredients

- **1 cup Pamela's Baking & Pancake Mix (or similar brown rice mix)**
- **1 large egg or egg alternative* (V)**
- **3/4 cup water**
- **1 Tbsp. coconut oil**

Directions

1. Follow the pancake directions on the back of the mix.
2. Use coconut oil for the mix and to cook the pancakes.
3. Serve with Fresh Berry Syrup.
4. Note: Add more water to batter for thinner pancakes. Less water for thicker pancakes.

*EASY EGG ALTERNATIVE

(THIS VEGAN EGG SUBSTITUTION IS EQUAL TO 1 EGG.)

- **1 Tbsp. ground flax seeds**
- **3 Tbsp. water**
- **Stir together until thick and gelatinous.**

BLUEBERRY PITBULL PANCAKES

(V, G, H, A) | SERVES 4-5

Ingredients

1 cup Pamela's Baking & Pancake Mix (or similar brown rice mix)

1 large egg or egg alternative* (V)

3/4 cup water

1 Tbsp. coconut oil

1 1/2 cups fresh blueberries (mix into batter before pouring into pan)

Directions

1. Follow the pancake directions on the back of the mix.
2. Use coconut oil for the mix and to cook the pancakes.
3. Serve with Fresh Berry Syrup.
4. Note: Add more water to batter for thinner pancakes. Less water for thicker pancakes.

*EASY EGG ALTERNATIVE

(THIS EGG SUBSTITUTION IS EQUAL TO 1 EGG.)

1 Tbsp. ground flax seeds

3 Tbsp. water

Stir together until thick and gelatinous.

BANANA FLAXSEED PITBULL PANCAKES

(V, G, H, A) | SERVES 4-5

Ingredients

1 cup Pamela's Baking & Pancake Mix (or similar brown rice mix)

1 large egg or egg alternative* (V)

3/4 cup water

1 Tbsp. coconut oil

2 bananas, chopped (add to batter before pouring into pan)

1/2 cup ground flaxseed (add to batter before pouring into pan)

dash of cinnamon

Directions

1. Follow the pancake directions on the back of the mix.
2. Use coconut oil for the mix and to cook the pancakes.
3. Serve with Fresh Berry Syrup.

Note: Add more water to batter for thinner pancakes. Less water for thicker pancakes.

*EASY EGG ALTERNATIVE

(THIS EGG SUBSTITUTION IS EQUAL TO 1 EGG.)

1 Tbsp. ground flax seeds

3 Tbsp. water

Stir together until thick and gelatinous.

FRESH BERRY SYRUP

(V, G, H, A) | SERVES 4-5

Note: Pairs with pancakes, East Coast Breakfast Toast, plain Greek yogurt, cereals & more!

Ingredients

4 oz. water

1 cup strawberries

1 cup blueberries

1 Tbsp. agave (optional)

Directions

1. Add water and fruit to small saucepan.

2. Cover and turn to low-medium heat.

3. When fruit softens, reduce heat and mash with spatula.

4. Add agave, stir and serve.

FETA, SPINACH & TOMATO EGG SCRAMBLE

(G, H, A) | SERVES 1

Ingredients

2 whole eggs

3-4 Tbsp. almond milk

large handful baby spinach

1 Tbsp. feta

1 small vine-ripened tomato, seeded & diced

2 Tbsp. grapeseed oil

2 Tbsp. red beans (optional)

dash of black pepper

Directions

1. Heat grapeseed oil in medium pan on low.
2. Whisk eggs and milk together in small bowl and add to pan, stirring frequently.
3. When eggs are still a bit runny, add in spinach and beans, and continue mixing. Spinach will wilt as eggs cook.
4. Once done, spoon eggs onto small plate and top with diced tomatoes, black pepper and feta.

BREAKFAST BOWL

(V, G, H, A) | SERVES 1-2

Ingredients

1/2 cup oat bran or buckwheat (G)

1/4 cup blueberries

1/2 cup strawberries

1/4 cup raisins

1/2 sliced banana

1 Tbsp. all-natural peanut butter or almond butter

1 Tbsp. ground flaxseeds

1 pinch cinnamon

1 cup water

Directions

1. In a medium saucepan, bring 1 cup water to boil.
2. Reduce flame and mix in berries and oat bran, stirring often until desired consistency is reached.
3. Mix in flaxseeds, raisins and cinnamon.
4. Pour into bowl and add peanut butter or almond butter and top with banana.
5. Add in a dash of almond milk or water to thin out oat bran if desired.

EAST COAST BREAKFAST TOAST

(V, G, H, A) | SERVES 1

Ingredients

> **1 egg (or egg alternative)**
>
> **1/4 cup almond milk**
>
> **2 slices bread**
>
> **coconut oil (as needed)**
>
> **dash of cinnamon**

Directions

1. Coat pan with coconut oil and place over low heat.
2. In bowl, beat eggs and milk together with fork.
3. Dip bread slices into egg mixture and soak through.
4. Put bread slices in pan and heat until lightly browned.
5. Be sure to flip them over to cook both sides.
6. Repeat until all bread slices have been browned.
7. Top each bread slice with cinnamon and fresh fruit, or serve with Fresh Berry Syrup.

Note: If cooking for more than one person, simply double the recipe as you see fit.

OATS & BERRIES SMOOTHIE

(V, G, H, A) | SERVES 1-2

Note: There are more smoothie recipes later in the book!

Ingredients

1 cup blueberries

1 cup strawberries

1 orange

1 banana

1/2 cup uncooked oat bran or buckwheat (G)

1/2 cup almond milk

1 tsp. agave

1 tsp. ground flaxseed

10 ice cubes

Directions

Combine in blender and blend until creamy.

TOFU VEGGIE SCRAMBLE

(V, G, H, A)　|　SERVES 4-6

Ingredients

2 (15 oz.) packages firm tofu

1 Tbsp. grapeseed oil

3 green onions, chopped

3 garlic cloves, minced

1 Tbsp. fresh squeezed lime juice

1/2 green bell pepper, chopped

1/2 red bell pepper, chopped

4 sprays of Bragg Liquid Aminos (or 2 Tbsp. low-sodium soy sauce)

3/4 cup salsa (see homemade recipe for salsa in Snack section)

1/4 cup cilantro, chopped

dash of black pepper, to taste

Directions

1. Drain tofu, pat dry and grate into large bowl.

2. In large pan, sauté onions, garlic and bell peppers on medium heat in grapeseed oil until tender. Mix in the grated tofu and cook another 5 minutes, stirring often.

3. Now add in lime juice, Bragg's Liquid Aminos, salsa and cilantro and mix well.

4. Serve over leafy greens, or whole wheat or gluten-free toast.

ALMOND BUTTER & FRUIT PITA

(V, G, H, A) | SERVES 1

Ingredients

1/2 banana, sliced

1/4 cup fresh strawberries, sliced

2 pieces of your favorite whole wheat or gluten-free pita bread

2 Tbsp. almond butter

Directions

1. Split pita bread open and toast.
2. Smear almond butter inside and pack with banana and strawberry slices.

Note: Apple slices also taste great!

LUNCH

THE GREEN REUBEN

(G, H, A) | SERVES 1

Ingredients

Reuben Dressing (recipe follows - make this first)

2 slices whole wheat or gluten-free bread

1 Tbsp. mustard

1/4 cup Eden Organic Sauerkraut (or similar)

2 slices of Swiss cheese

1/2 avocado

2 Tbsp. grapeseed oil

Directions

1. Spread one slice of bread with some mustard, the other slice with Reuben Dressing.
2. Drizzle grapeseed oil into, and then add in bread slices, dry side down.
3. Top one slice with avocado and Swiss cheese, and the other with sauerkraut.
4. Over medium heat, grill the sandwich until browned, about 5 minutes.
5. Put the sandwich halves together and enjoy!

REUBEN DRESSING

(G, H, A) | SERVES 1

Ingredients

4 Tbsp. Vegenaise

1 1/2 Tbsp. ketchup

1 Tbsp. horseradish

1/2 tsp. sweet pickle relish

dash of Worcestershire sauce

Directions

1. Blend the ingredients thoroughly in a bowl.
2. Spread on bread slice to complete your Green Reuben.
3. Enjoy!

WARM QUINOA, CHICKPEA & VEGGIE BOWL

(V, G, H, A) | SERVES 2-4

Ingredients

- **1 cup quinoa**
- **1 Tbsp. grapeseed oil**
- **1 red bell pepper**
- **1 green bell pepper**
- **3/4 cup chickpeas**
- **about 14 cherry tomatoes**
- **1/4 cup red onion, chopped**

Directions

1. Cook quinoa according to package directions and set aside to cool.
2. Slice peppers and onions and sauté in grapeseed oil for a few minutes until soft.
3. Toss tomatoes into the pan with the peppers/onions mix. Sauté for another 2-3 minutes until tomato skin begin to crumple.
4. Now add in chickpeas and sauté another minute.
5. Time to serve! Scoop quinoa into individual serving bowls and then top with veggie mixture.
6. Enjoy!

APPLE, RAISIN & CARROT JUBILEE

(V, G, H, A) | SERVES 2

Ingredients

3 large carrots, grated

1/2 cup chopped cashews (put them in a Ziploc bag & smash them with a meat mallet)

2 apples, cubed

1/2 cup raisins

1 Tbsp. lemon juice

2 Tbsp. Vegenaise

dash of sea salt

dash of black pepper

1 Tbsp. olive oil

Directions:

Put ingredients in a big bowl and mix well. Serve and enjoy!

QUINOA SOUTHWEST SALAD

(V, G, H, A) | SERVES 2-4

Ingredients

- **1 cup quinoa**
- **1 can black beans (drained)**
- **2 garlic cloves, minced**
- **1/2 cup celery, chopped**
- **1 carrot, diced**
- **1 cup fresh green beans, chopped**
- **1/2 cup red bell pepper, diced**
- **1/2 cup green bell pepper, diced**
- **1 medium vine-ripened tomato, sliced**
- **1 cup cucumber, chopped**
- **1/4 cup sliced olives**
- **2 Tbsp. fresh basil, chopped**
- **1/4 cup green onions, chopped**
- **2 Tbsp. grapeseed oil**
- **3 Tbsp. extra virgin olive oil (for dressing)**

Directions

1. Cook quinoa according to package directions and set aside.
2. Together, sauté garlic, carrot, peppers, green beans and celery in 2 Tbsp. of grapeseed oil for about 5 minutes until soft.
3. Transfer quinoa and veggies to large bowl and mix.
4. Add in all additional ingredients and mix thoroughly.
5. Dish into individual serving bowls and drizzle with extra virgin olive oil.

CRANBERRY CASHEW SPINACH SALAD

(V, G, H, A) | SERVES 2-4

Ingredients

3 large handfuls organic spinach (about 3-4 oz.)

1 shallot, chopped

1/4 cup balsamic vinegar

1/4 cup extra virgin olive oil

dash of sea salt

dash of black pepper

1 Tbsp. spicy brown or Dijon mustard

1 cup dried cranberries

1 cup cashews, crushed or whole

PHOTO: EMILE VASILEV

Directions

1. For the dressing, whisk together the chopped shallot pieces, mustard, balsamic vinegar, sea salt and pepper.

2. Then toss the spinach leaves with dressing and mix in the cranberries and pecans.

3. Enjoy!

SANTORINI ISLAND SALAD

(V, G, H, A) | SERVES 2-4

Ingredients

4 cups arugula & spinach mix

1/4 cup feta cheese crumbles

1 red onion, chopped

2 pieces of celery chopped

1 1/2 cups chickpeas

1/2 cup black pitted olives

1/2 cucumber, peeled & chopped

Directions

Put into large bowl and mix well. Top with Santorini Dressing below.

SANTORINI ISLAND DRESSING

SERVES 2

Ingredients

1 Tbsp. apple cider vinegar

3 sun-dried tomatoes, chopped

3 Tbsp. extra virgin olive oil

1 garlic clove, minced

1 lemon (juice & zest)

zest is grated lemon peel

salt & pepper to taste

Directions

Put ingredients in a bowl, whisk together until smooth and mix into salad.

CINNAMON APPLE GRILLED CHEESE

(G, H, A) | SERVES 1

Ingredients

2 slices whole wheat or gluten-free bread

1 organic red apple, thinly sliced

2 Tbsp. maple syrup (agave also works well here)

dash of cinnamon

1 Tbsp. grapeseed oil

2 Tbsp. feta cheese crumbles

Directions

1. Lightly coat small pan with grapeseed oil and put on medium heat.

2. Place apple slices in pan. Apples can be touching but not on top of each other.

3. Drizzle small amount of maple syrup on each slice (not more than 2 Tbsp. worth for the whole pan) and then dash with cinnamon.

4. Cook for about 2 minutes, then flip and cook for additional 2 minutes until lightly browned around edges.

5. When apples are almost done, lightly toast bread slices.

6. Place apples on one side of bread, followed by a layer of feta crumbles and then another layer of hot apple slices. Top with remaining bread slice. Enjoy!

HOT AVOCADO CHICKEN SANDWICH

(G, H, A) | SERVES 1

Ingredients

2 slices whole wheat or gluten-free bread

1 slice cheddar, or cheese of your choice

1 chicken breast, cooked & chopped

1 Tbsp. green pepper, minced

1 Tbsp. onion, minced

1 Tbsp. Vegenaise

3 thin avocado slices

2 Tbsp. grapeseed oil (for sautéing)

PHOTO: SARAH BALLANTYNE

Directions

1. Chop chicken, peppers and onions and sauté in separate pans in grapeseed oil. (Chicken in one pan, veggies in the other.)

2. Make sure to cook onions and green peppers until soft.

3. Slice avocado pieces and set aside.

4. When chicken and veggies are nearly done, toast your bread.

5. As soon as bread is done, spread Vegenaise onto slices, then lay down the avocado, then cheese and top with hot chicken and veggies. Top with other bread slice, mash down and enjoy!

BACON, SPINACH & TOMATO SANDWICH

(G, H, A) | SERVES 1

Ingredients

2 slices of whole wheat or gluten-free bread

2 slices low-sodium turkey bacon

small handful of fresh spinach leaves

1/2 vine-ripe tomato, thinly sliced

1 Tbsp. Vegenaise

Directions

1. Cook turkey bacon in a pan with grapeseed oil until crispy, then place on paper towels. Once cool enough, break each bacon piece in half and set aside.

2. Lightly toast bread, then smear with Vegenaise.

3. Place tomato slices, followed by spinach then bacon pieces on one bread slice and top with remaining piece of bread.

4. Cut in half or quarters and enjoy!

HONEY MUSTARD TURKEY & PEAR SALAD

(G, H, A) | SERVES 2-4

Ingredients

1 organic turkey breast (not deli slices)

2 large handfuls arugula & spinach mix

1 pear, sliced into thin, flat pieces

1 Tbsp. apple cider vinegar

3 Tbsp. extra virgin olive oil

1 Tbsp. feta crumbles or 2 slices provolone (optional)

1 Tbsp. Annie's Organic Honey Mustard

Directions

1. Slice raw turkey breast and brush with honey mustard. Cook in pan with grapeseed oil.

2. Layer pear slices on turkey pieces in pan. Follow with layer of cheese.

3. Cover and cook about 3 minutes until cheese melts.

4. Place spinach and arugula mix into bowls and place turkey slices on top.

5. Dressing: Whisk a Tbsp. of the honey mustard with a Tbsp. of olive oil and drizzle onto salad.

HONEY CHICKEN LETTUCE CUPS

(G, H, A) | SERVES 4-6

Ingredients

10 large butter lettuce leaves

8-10 sprays of Bragg Liquid Aminos to taste (or 2 Tbsp. low-sodium soy sauce)

3 Tbsp. honey

2 Tbsp. apple cider vinegar

4 Tbsp. peanut oil

3 boneless skinless chicken breasts, chopped

dash of black pepper

2 garlic cloves, finely chopped

1 Tbsp. ginger root, grated

1 bunch scallions, diced

8 oz. water chestnuts, drained

1/4 cup roasted unsalted cashews, crushed

1 tsp. sesame seeds

1 cup quinoa (optional)

HONEY CHICKEN LETTUCE CUPS

(V,G, H, A) | SERVES 4

Directions

1. Sprinkle the chicken pieces with pepper and cook it in the peanut oil on medium to high heat, stirring occasionally.

2. Add 2 Tbsp. peanut oil to separate large pan and stir in the grated ginger, garlic and scallions.

3. In about 2 minutes, add in water chestnuts, cashews and the honey mixture. Sauté together for about 2-3 minutes and then reduce to a simmer.

4. Once the chicken is done, drain juices from pan and add the chicken to the veggie pan. Mix everything together thoroughly. Remove from heat.

5. Put mixture in serving bowl and the lettuce leaves on a plate. To serve, spoon the chicken into each lettuce leaf, wrap the leaf around the chicken mixture, and enjoy!

TUNA-STUFFED TOMATOES

(G, H, A) | SERVES 1-2

Ingredients

2 large vine-ripened tomatoes

1 can tuna in water, drained

2 Tbsp. Vegenaise

dash of sea salt

dash of black pepper

Directions

1. Wash and core tomatoes and set aside.
2. In a small bowl, combine tuna, Vegenaise, salt and pepper and mix well.
3. Stuff tuna mixture into tomatoes.
4. Enjoy!

PHENOM CHICKEN & DATE WRAPS

(G, H, A) | SERVES 2-4

Ingredients

- **2-4 whole wheat or gluten-free wraps**
- **1 chicken breast**
- **8 dates, pitted & sliced**
- **8 oz. small curd plain cottage cheese**
- **2 Tbsp. grapeseed oil**

Directions

1. Slice chicken breast into thin strips and cook in grapeseed oil and set aside.
2. Spread thin layer of cottage cheese on wraps and line with dates and chicken strips.
3. Wrap and eat!

ZUCCHINI, BLACK BEAN & QUINOA SOUP

(G, H, A) | SERVES 4-6

Ingredients

- **6 cups low-sodium chicken broth**
- **1 cup uncooked quinoa**
- **1 large onion, sliced**
- **1 1/2 cups black beans**
- **2 large carrots, chopped**
- **3 cloves garlic, minced**
- **3 Tbsp. grapeseed oil**
- **1 lb. zucchini, chopped**
- **1 lb. kale leaves, chopped**
- **dash of sea salt**
- **dash of black pepper**

Directions

1. In a large pot bring chicken broth to a boil and add in quinoa. Lower to a simmer and cover. Cook for about 30-40 minutes or until quinoa is soft.
2. Meanwhile, in large pan, sauté onions, carrots and garlic in grapeseed oil until tender.
3. Add in zucchini and cook about 5 minutes.
4. Mix in kale and cook until wilted, then set aside.
5. When quinoa is soft, stir in black beans along with veggie mixture.
6. Season with salt and pepper. The soup should be pretty thick. You can thin it out with additional broth if you'd like.
7. Enjoy!

CASHEW & MINT QUINOA

(V, G, H, A) | SERVES 4-6

Ingredients

1 cup quinoa

1 cup cashews, crushed

2 Tbsp. extra virgin olive oil

1/2 cup black beans

1/2 cup chickpeas

1/2 cup scallions, chopped

1/4 cup mint, chopped

1 cup cauliflower, finely chopped

1/2 cup carrots, finely chopped

PHOTO: EMILE VASILEV

Directions

1. Cook quinoa according to package directions and set aside.
2. Sauté carrots and cauliflower until tender.
3. Combine all ingredients in large bowl and serve.

MAPLE CHICKEN VEGGIE KABOBS

(G, H, A) | SERVES 4-6

Ingredients

1 1/2 lbs. skinless boneless chicken breast, cut into 2-inch chunks

12 skewers

1 tsp. sea salt

1 large red bell pepper, seeded & cut into 2-inch slices

1 large green bell pepper, seeded & cut into 2-inch slices

7 oz. Portabella mushrooms, cut into chunks (optional)

1 bottle Annie's Organic Smoky Maple BBQ Sauce (or similar)

Directions

1. The key to the kabob is to cut everything so that you can spear it with a stick!

2. You can make this on the grill or in the oven. If using oven, preheat to 350 degrees.

3. In bowl, coat chicken chunks with about 3/4 cup of the Annie's Maple BBQ Sauce, cover and let marinate about 15-20 minutes.

4. Then, in large pan, sear all sides of the chicken pieces so that when skewered, no raw chicken is touching the veggies.

5. Skewer the chicken and all veggies and place on grill, turning occasionally until chicken is cooked through and veggies are browned at edges. If cooking in oven, you'll need one large (or multiple) baking dish(es).

6. Place skewers in baking dishes, brush chicken and veggies with sauce and cook for about 30 minutes or until chicken pieces are cooked through and veggies are browned at edges.

7. Whether you're cooking these on the grill or in the oven, be sure to baste occasionally while cooking.

8. Serve and enjoy!

ITALIAN CHICKEN KABOBS

(G, H, A) | SERVES 4-6

This is similar process as the previous kabob recipe except the marinade is different.

Ingredients

1 1/2 lbs. skinless boneless chicken breast, cut into 2-inch chunks

12 skewers

2 Tbsp. apple cider vinegar

1 1/2 tsp. sea salt

1/2 tsp. hot red pepper flakes (optional)

1 Tbsp. extra virgin olive oil

1 Tbsp. fresh basil, chopped

1 Tbsp. fresh oregano, chopped

2 garlic cloves, minced

2 zucchini, sliced into rounds

1 large red bell pepper, seeded & cut into 2-inch slices

1 large green bell pepper, seeded & cut into 2-inch slices

7 oz. Portabella mushrooms, cut into chunks (optional)

Directions

1. The key to the kabob is cut everything so that you can spear it with a stick!

2. You can make this on the grill or in the oven. If using oven, preheat to 350 degrees.

3. Whisk apple cider vinegar, 1 tsp. sea salt, and hot red pepper in bowl, followed by olive oil. Add basil, oregano and garlic, and stir. Add in chicken and toss to coat. Let marinate about 15-20 minutes.

4. In large pan, sear all sides of the chicken pieces so that when skewered, no raw chicken is touching the veggies.

5. Skewer the chicken and all veggies and place on grill, turning occasionally until chicken is cooked through and veggies are browned at edges. If cooking in oven, you'll need one large (or multiple) baking dish(es).

6. Place skewers in baking dishes, brush chicken and veggies with sauce and cook for about 30 minutes or until chicken pieces are cooked through and veggies are browned at edges.

7. Whether you're cooking these on the grill or in the oven, be sure to baste occasionally while cooking. Serve and enjoy!

HOMEMADE REFRIED BEAN TACOS

(V, G, H, A) | SERVES 4-6

Ingredients

1 15 oz. can pinto beans, drained

1/2 cup aged cheddar, shredded (optional)

dash of sea salt

6 organic taco shells (choose gluten-free shells if you'd like)

splash of water

1 small onion, diced

large handful of spinach, shredded

2 small tomatoes, diced

Directions

1. In small pan, sauté onions until tender.

2. In small pot add pinto beans, onions, splash of water, dash of sea salt and a sprinkle of the cheddar cheese and put on low heat.

3. Mash bean mixture with potato masher or fork, and crush and mix until smooth. (You can also use an electric mixer or food processor here and then add the mixture to the pot to warm.)

4. Once smooth and heated, spoon beans into taco shells.

5. Top with spinach, tomato and leftover shredded cheese.

CHICKEN APPLE QUESADILLAS

(G, H, A) | Serves 2-4

Ingredients

4 gluten-free tortillas

1 chicken breast, cooked & shredded

1 cup aged white cheddar (optional) or nutritional yeast

1 apple, sliced thin

Directions

1. In large pan, warm one tortilla at a time, sprinkle each with cheese a scoop of shredded chicken and a thin layer of apples.

2. Fold tortilla in half and flip over to cook other side.

3. When cheese melts remove from pan and cut in triangles.

QUINOA VEGGIE BAKE

(V, G, H, A) | SERVES 4-6

Ingredients

1 cup quinoa, cooked according to package directions & set aside

1 bunch of baby broccoli, chopped

1 cup carrots, finely diced

2 cloves garlic, minced

1 Tbsp. Vegenaise

1/2 cup nutritional yeast (or Parmesan cheese)

dash of sea salt, to taste

dash of pepper, to taste

Directions

1. Preheat oven to 350 degrees.

2. Combine cooked quinoa and rest of ingredients in casserole dish and top with a few more sprinkles of nutritional yeast (or Parmesan cheese).

3. Bake 20 minutes.

4. Enjoy!

DOLCE FETA PIZZA

(G, H, A) | SERVES 2

Ingredients

1 gluten-free or whole wheat pizza crust

handful kale

1 small onion, chopped

1 15 oz. can diced tomatoes

2 Tbsp. grapeseed oil

dash of Italian herb seasoning

1 cup feta cheese crumbles

Directions

1. Preheat oven to 350 degrees.

2. Sauté onions in grapeseed oil until tender.

3. Add in handful of kale and mix with onions until wilted.

4. Spread diced tomatoes and their juices over pizza crust, careful to leave the edge of the crust plain.

5. Spread onion and kale mixture.

6. Sprinkle feta crumbles evenly over pizza.

7. Sprinkle on herb seasoning.

8. Cook for 30 minutes, or until edges of pizza crust brown.

9. Enjoy!

OPEN-FACE TURKEY SALAD SANDWICH

(G, H, A) | SERVES 4

Ingredients

8 slices whole wheat or gluten-free bread, lightly toasted

2 fresh turkey breasts (not deli slices)

2 Tbsp. olive oil

2 cups seedless red grapes, halved

2 apples, chopped

6 cups fresh baby spinach

2 Tbsp. apple cider vinegar

4 pieces provolone, thinly sliced

Directions

1. Thinly slice turkey breast and cook in grapeseed oil. Layer provolone slice over turkey breast, then set aside.

2. In pan, lightly sauté grapes and apples in grapeseed oil for about 1-2 minutes.

3. Place two pieces of bread on a plate and layer with turkey slices, apple and grape mixture, spinach and drizzle with apple cider vinegar.

SALMON & GREENS SALAD

(G, H, A) | SERVES 1

Ingredients

4 oz. Wild Alaska Salmon (canned, water drained)

large handful baby spinach

1/4 cup black beans

2 Tbsp. extra virgin olive oil

1/4 cup raisins

Optional: Add 1 or 2 hard-boiled eggs to the salad to beef it up.

Directions

1. In bowl, combine spinach, raisins and chickpeas.
2. In small pot, slowly warm the salmon and then add into salad.
3. Drizzle olive oil over top of salad. Enjoy!

HONEY, YAM & BEAN WRAP

(G, H, A) | SERVES 4-6

Ingredients

8 whole wheat or gluten-free wraps

2 large yams, peeled & cut into chunks

4 Tbsp. grapeseed oil

1/2 yellow onion, diced

2 cups cooked black beans, rinsed & drained

1/2 tsp. ground cumin

dash of sea salt, to taste

dash of black pepper, to taste

drizzle of honey

Directions

1. Preheat oven to 375 degrees.
2. In large mixing bowl, toss yam chunks with 3 Tbsp. of grapeseed oil.
3. Spread coated yams on baking sheet and cook for 20 minutes or until tender.
4. In large pan, add 1 Tbsp. grapeseed oil and sauté onion until tender.
5. Add beans, cumin, salt and pepper to onion pan and stir well.
6. Remove from heat and mix in cooked yams.
7. Spoon mixture into wraps, drizzle with honey, fold up and enjoy!

BLACK BEAN & ZUCCHINI QUESADILLAS

(V, G, H, A) | SERVES 2

Ingredients

1/2 cup canned black beans, rinsed & drained

2 Tbsp. salsa (Fresh Salsa recipe is in the Sides & Snacks section)

1/2 cup zucchini, peeled & finely chopped

4 whole wheat or gluten-free wraps

1/4 cup aged cheddar cheese (optional)

Directions

1. Preheat oven to 350 degrees.

2. Combine beans and salsa in a small bowl; mash with a fork and then mix in zucchini.

3. Layer 1 wrap with half the bean mixture, sprinkle with some cheese, and then top with another wrap.

4. Repeat this process with the remaining wraps.

5. Place wraps on a baking sheet and cook for about 2 minutes on each side until the cheese is melted and wraps are lightly browned.

6. Enjoy!

WARM APPLE QUINOA

(V, G, H, A) | SERVES 1-2

Ingredients

1/2 cup quinoa, cooked

1/4 cup unsweetened almond milk

1 apple, chopped

1/4 tsp. vanilla extract

dash of Saigon cinnamon

Directions

Mix ingredients in small pot and heat until warm.
Serve and enjoy!

MIKE'S AVOCADO SALMON SALAD

(G, H, A) | SERVES 2-4

Ingredients

1 6-oz. can wild-caught Alaskan Sockeye

1/2 stalk celery, chopped

1/4 cup red or sweet onion, chopped

2 tsp. spicy brown mustard or horseradish

2 Tbsp. dill pickle relish (unsweetened)

1/4 tsp. black pepper

7 pitted black olives, chopped (optional)

1/2 avocado

brown rice wrap or bread

Directions

1. Put salmon in a large mixing bowl and mix in celery, onion, mustard, relish, olives, pepper and avocado.

2. Mix thoroughly, stirring avocado into the mixture.

3. Transfer salad to brown rice wrap or bread.

4. Enjoy!

CHICKPEA SALAD

(V, G, H, A) | SERVES 2

Ingredients

6 oz. chickpeas (garbanzo beans)

handful baby spinach

handful kale

1/2 cucumber, sliced

1/4 chopped onion

1/2 tomato, chopped (or 6 cherry tomatoes)

1/2 cup chopped walnuts

6 sliced strawberries

4 oz. feta cheese crumbles (optional)

3 Tbsp. extra virgin olive oil

3 Tbsp. balsamic vinegar

Directions

Combine all ingredients in bowl and drizzle with olive oil and balsamic vinegar.

EGG SALAD

(G, H, A) | SERVES 2

Ingredients

4 whole hard-boiled eggs, peeled & chopped

1/4 onion, chopped

1 celery stalk, chopped

dash sea salt

dash black pepper

1 avocado

bread or wrap

PHOTO: CHRISTINE ASHTON

Shown topped with cayenne
pepper and almonds

Directions

1. Combine eggs, onion, celery, salt and pepper in mixing bowl

2. Scoop out whole avocado and add to mixture.

3. Mash well.

4. Serve on whole wheat or gluten-free bread, in wrap or over salad.

TUNA SALAD

(G, H, A) | SERVES 2

Ingredients

- **1 can tuna in water**
- **1/4 onion, chopped**
- **1/2 celery stalk, chopped**
- **1/2 avocado**
- **1-2 Tbsp. brown spicy mustard**
- **1 Tbsp. sweet pickle relish**
- **1 hard-boiled egg**

Directions

Mix all ingredients together and put on whole wheat or gluten-free bread, in wrap or enjoy over green salad.

SUPAFLY
CHICKEN SALAD
(G, H, A) | SERVES 2·

Ingredients

8 oz. chicken breast, cut into bite-sized pieces

1/2 celery stalk, chopped

1 cup grapes, halved

1 cup chickpeas

1 avocado, peeled & pitted

1 tsp. lemon juice

sea salt & pepper, to taste

Directions

1. Lightly coat pan with grapeseed oil and cook chicken over low-medium heat.

2. Combine rest of ingredients in large bowl and mix well, mashing avocado into mixture.

3. Once chicken is cooked, let cool and then add to rest of ingredients in bowl and mix well.

4. Chill until serving.

5. This salad can be served a number of ways: on a bed of lettuce, on whole grain bread or in a gluten-free wrap.

STRAWBERRY SALAD

(V, G, H, A) | SERVES 1-2

Ingredients

2 handfuls baby spinach

10 fresh strawberries, sliced

1/2 avocado, cut into bite-sized chunks

1 cup walnuts

Directions

Arrange spinach, avocado, walnuts and strawberries in bowl.

Dressing: light drizzle of extra virgin olive oil and balsamic vinegar

PASTA SALAD WITH VEGGIES

(V, G, H, A) | SERVES 2-4

Ingredients

2 cups rotini pasta or gluten-free pasta, cooked according to package instructions & drained

1 cup chopped broccoli, steamed

1 cup chickpeas

1/3 cup cubed or shredded mozzarella cheese (optional)

1 clove garlic, minced

1/2 tomato, diced

Directions

In a bowl, mix all ingredients together. Cool in refrigerator until ready to serve. To serve, add dressing and cheese.

Dressing: light drizzle of extra virgin olive oil & balsamic vinegar

SIMPLE SPINACH SALAD

(V, G, H, A) | SERVES 1

Note: This is a great weight-cutting meal when you need to be light but want to keep your energy high.

Ingredients

handful fresh spinach leaves

handful brightly colored vegetables of your choice, chopped

handful fruit, chopped

Directions

Mix all ingredients in bowl and top with dressing.

Dressing: light drizzle of hemp oil & apple cider vinegar

WALDORF SALAD

(G, H, A)　|　SERVES 2-4

Ingredients

1/2 cup chopped walnuts

1/2 cup plain yogurt

2 Tbsp. avocado

2 Tbsp. parsley, minced

1 tsp. honey

freshly ground black pepper to taste

2 large apples, chopped into 1/2-inch pieces

2 celery stalks, chopped

1/4 cup raisins

1/2 lemon, juiced

1 head Romaine lettuce, shredded into bite-sized pieces

Directions

1. Mix yogurt, avocado, parsley, honey and pepper in a bowl.
2. Add the apples, celery and raisins and sprinkle with the lemon juice; toss with yogurt mixture.
3. Wait to add walnuts and lettuce until you're ready to eat the salad.
4. Chill before serving.

ADDITIONAL DRESSINGS

OIL & VINEGAR DRESSING

extra virgin olive oil, add to taste
balsamic vinegar, add to taste

NATURE'S DRESSING

hemp oil, add to taste
apple cider vinegar, add to taste

GRAPESEED PESTO

Ingredients

1 1/2 cups fresh basil leaves

1/2 cup grapeseed oil

Grind basil to a fine paste with mortar and pestle* and put in small bowl.

Add grapeseed oil and stir.

Directions

*You can also use a blender or food processor.

STRAWBERRY VINAIGRETTE

Ingredients

1/2 cup extra virgin olive oil

1/2 pint fresh strawberries, halved

2 Tbsp. balsamic vinegar

1/2 tsp. sea salt

1/4 tsp. black pepper

Directions

Blend all ingredients until smooth. Serve over salad.

DINNER

SLIGHTLY SLOPPY MIKES

(G, H, A) | SERVES 4

Ingredients

whole wheat or gluten-free buns (regular bread slices will do just fine, too!)

1/2 lb. organic ground turkey

1 small onion, finely chopped

2 cloves garlic, minced

1 green bell pepper, diced

1/2 cup pinto beans

1/2 cup black beans

1 cup diced tomatoes

1/2 Tbsp. tomato paste

1/2 Tbsp. apple cider vinegar

1 Tbsp. maple syrup

1 Tbsp. Worcestershire sauce

1 Tbsp. spicy mustard

dash of sea salt

dash of black pepper

1 jalapeño pepper, minced (optional)

Directions

1. Cook turkey meat on medium heat for about 10 minutes until done.

2. In separate, large pan, sauté onion, garlic, green pepper and jalapeño until soft.

3. Add meat to the veggie pan along with rest of ingredients and reduce heat to a simmer, stirring occasionally.

4. Once thickened, scoop onto bread of your choice and serve.

5. This can also be eaten breadless in a bowl!

STEAK & ASPARAGUS
(G, H, A) | Serves 2-4

Note: This can be served on a bed of quinoa.

Ingredients

3 Tbsp. grapeseed oil

4 cloves garlic, minced

1 large sirloin steak, cut into 1/2 inch cubes

3-4 sprays of Bragg's Liquid Aminos or 1 Tbsp. low-sodium soy sauce

1 medium yellow onion, diced

2 stalks celery, diced

5 oz. crimini mushrooms, sliced

1 lb. asparagus, each spear chopped into 1/2-inch bites

1/2 cup water

Directions

1. Heat grapeseed oil in a large pan over medium heat and spray steak with Braggs Liquid Aminos or low-sodium soy sauce. Cook until steak is browned on all sides, about 3 minutes. Turn off heat and set aside.

2. In separate pan, add garlic, onion, celery and sliced asparagus. Sauté 2 minutes and add steak into mixture. Add water and cover pan. Cook about 5 minutes or until asparagus is tender and steak pieces are cooked through. Enjoy!

THE CHICKEN BURGER

(G, H, A) | SERVES 2-4

Ingredients

1 lb. ground chicken

1 shallot, diced

1 Tbsp. garlic, minced

1/2 cup crimini mushrooms

1 egg

4 Tbsp. grapeseed oil

1 green bell pepper, chopped

4 whole wheat or gluten-free buns (or go protein style & wrap in butter lettuce leaves!)

large handful baby spinach leaves

1 large avocado, sliced

1 large vine-ripened tomato, sliced

1/2 cup oat bran (or buckwheat for gluten-free option)

1 tsp. sea salt

1 Tbsp. black pepper

Directions

1. In large pan, add 2 Tbsp. grapeseed oil and sauté the shallot, bell pepper and garlic until tender.

2. Add in the mushrooms and stir for about 2 minutes or until mushrooms brown. Set aside and let vegetables cool.

3. Next, in a large bowl, combine the chicken, vegetables, egg, oat bran, salt and pepper.

4. Mix all ingredients together and form into 8 patties.

5. Heat 2 Tbsp. grapeseed oil in large pan and cook each chicken patty over medium heat for about 5 minutes on each side until cooked through.

6. Place burger on buns or lettuce leaves and top with tomato, avocado and spinach. Add ketchup or mustard to taste.

THE EMPEROR'S NEW SALAD

Black Rice with Roasted Baby Broccoli, Feta

(G, H, A) | SERVES 2-4

Ingredients

- 1/2 cup black rice
- 1 1/4 cups low-sodium chicken broth
- 1 onion, diced
- 2 cloves garlic, chopped
- 8 oz. crimini mushrooms, sliced
- 1 lb. baby broccoli, chopped
- handful dill, chopped
- 3 Tbsp. grapeseed oil (for use in sautéing)
- 1/4 cup grapeseed oil
- 2-3 Tbsp. apple cider vinegar, to taste
- 4 cups arugula & baby spinach, mixed
- 1/4 cup feta, crumbled
- sea salt, to taste
- pepper, to taste

Directions

1. Preheat oven to 400 degrees.

2. Bring the broth to a boil and add black rice. Reduce the heat and simmer covered, until the rice is tender, about 50 minutes.

3. In about 20 minutes, after rice is cooking, heat 2 Tbsp. grapeseed oil in pan and begin sautéing onion and garlic about 3-5 minutes. Add in mushrooms and sauté about 5 minutes until mushrooms are browned. Season with salt and pepper to taste and set aside.

4. While onion mixture is cooking, toss broccoli in a bowl with the rest of the grapeseed oil.

5. Spread the broccoli out on a baking dish and roast in oven until tender, about 10-15 minutes.

6. Mix the black rice, dill, and onion mixture, olive oil and apple cider vinegar.

7. Serve with black rice on a bed of spinach and arugula mix, topped with roasted broccoli and sprinkles of crumbled feta.

SPINACH & MUSHROOM LASAGNA

(G, H, A) | SERVES 4-6

Ingredients

1/2 lb. fresh mushrooms, sliced

1 tsp. chopped garlic

1/2 yellow onion, chopped

2 Tbsp. water

2 24-oz. jars of diced tomatoes

9-12 lasagna noodles (regular or no-boil is fine, uncooked)

Note: DeBoles makes a gluten-free rice lasagna.

2 Tbsp. grapeseed oil

5 oz. fresh baby spinach (about 2-3 large handfuls)

1 lb. cottage cheese

2 Tbsp. nutritional yeast (or Parmesan)

1/2 cup fresh mozzarella, shredded (optional)

1/2 tsp. garlic powder

2 Tbsp. Italian seasoning

Directions

1. Preheat oven to 350 degrees.

2. Sauté the mushrooms, onion and garlic over medium heat in grapeseed oil until tender. Add in spinach. When it begins to wilt, reduce heat to low and add tomatoes, stirring often. Cook about 3 minutes and set aside, covered.

3. In a large bowl, combine cottage cheese, nutritional yeast, Italian seasonings and garlic powder and mix well.

4. Spread a thin layer of tomato sauce in the bottom of a lasagna pan. This is our foundation.

5. Now place 3-4 lasagna noodles over the sauce. The noodles shouldn't overlap.

6. Next, spread a thin layer of cottage cheese mixture over the noodles.

7. Cover with another layer of 3-4 noodles followed by another layer of sauce and then another layer of cottage cheese. You should end up with a layer of noodles on top.

8. Spread the remaining tomato sauce on the top layer of noodles and sprinkle a few shakes of Italian seasoning on top.

9. Cover with aluminum foil, and bake for 40 minutes.

10. Remove the foil and sprinkle Parmesan or shredded mozzarella on top and bake uncovered for another 20 minutes.

11. Wait about 10-15 minutes before serving. Enjoy!

CLASSIC RED BEANS & RICE (WITH CHICKEN)

(V, G, H, A) | SERVES 4-6

Ingredients

2 chicken breasts, thinly sliced - or leave out (V)

1 yellow onion, diced

1 stalk celery, chopped

1 green pepper, diced

1 garlic clove, minced

1 Tbsp. grapeseed oil

3 (15-oz.) cans red beans, rinsed & drained

Note: Red beans & kidney beans are not the same, although one can be substituted for the other.

1 (16-oz.) can tomato paste

1 (14 1/2-oz.) can diced tomatoes

1 1/2 cups water

1/4 tsp. oregano

1/4 tsp. thyme

1/4 tsp. sage

1 Tbsp. parsley

dash of sea salt

dash of black pepper

1/4 tsp. Tabasco (optional)

1 bay leaf

1 cup brown rice, cooked according to package directions

Directions

1. Cook the chicken breast slices in one pan with grapeseed oil and set aside.

2. In another pan, cook the green pepper, celery, onion and garlic until vegetables are soft.

3. Now add the beans, tomato paste, tomatoes (with juice), water, all the spices, Tabasco and bay leaf.

4. Cook 10 minutes, stirring often. Reduce to a simmer, mix in chicken and cook another 10 minutes.

5. Remove bay leaf. Serve over rice (or quinoa). Enjoy!

BUCKWHEAT EGGPLANT PARMESAN

(V, G, H, A) | SERVES 2-4

Ingredients

1 large eggplant, peeled & cut into 1/4-inch round slices

2 eggs (V = use egg replacement)

1/4 cup almond milk

1 cup buckwheat

1 can diced tomatoes

4 Tbsp. grapeseed oil

1 1/2 cups fresh mozzarella, shredded (V = can substitute veggie cheese or nutritional yeast)

Directions

1. Preheat oven to 350 degrees.

2. Add grapeseed oil to large pan and put on low to medium heat.

3. Combine eggs and almond milk in small bowl and whisk together well.

4. Put buckwheat in a separate small bowl.

5. Dip each piece of eggplant (one at a time) first in the egg mixture and then in the buckwheat flakes and place into pan.

6. Cook the eggplant on both sides until tender and outsides are slightly browned.

7. Place eggplant in 9 x 12 casserole dish and cover with diced tomatoes and their juices.

8. Cover with aluminum foil and bake 30 minutes. Remove from oven, top with fresh mozzarella and put back in oven, uncovered, for about 10 minutes or until cheese is melted and slightly browned.

BUCKWHEAT CHICKEN PARMESAN

(G, H, A) | SERVES 2-4

Ingredients

2 chicken breasts, sliced thin

2 eggs

1/4 cup almond milk

1 cup buckwheat

1 can diced tomatoes

4 Tbsp. grapeseed oil

1 1/2 cup fresh mozzarella shredded*

***can substitute veggie cheese or nutritional yeast**

Directions

1. Preheat oven to 350 degrees.

2. Add grapeseed oil to large pan and put on low to medium heat.

3. Combine eggs and almond milk in small bowl and whisk together well.

4. Put buckwheat in a separate small bowl.

5. Dip each piece of chicken (one at a time) first in the egg mixture and then in the buckwheat flakes and place into pan.

6. Cook the chicken on both sides until tender and outsides are slightly browned.

7. Place chicken in 9 x 12 casserole dish and cover with diced tomatoes and their juices.

8. Cover with aluminum foil and bake 30 minutes. Remove from oven, top with fresh mozzarella and put back in oven, uncovered, for about 10 minutes or until cheese is melted and slightly browned.

COCONUT TROPICAL CHICKEN

(G, H, A) | Serves 2-4

Ingredients

2 chicken breasts, sliced in half lengthwise

2 eggs

1/4 cup almond milk

1/4 cup oat bran - or buckwheat (G)

1/4 cup ground flaxseed

1/4 cup unsweetened coconut flakes

4 Tbsp. unrefined coconut oil

Directions

1. Combine eggs and milk in one small bowl.

2. Combine flaxseed, coconut and oat bran in another small bowl.

3. Coat chicken first in the egg mixture and then roll it in the coconut mixture.

4. Place chicken pieces in large pan with coconut oil and cook on low to medium heat about 8-10 minutes, carefully flipping pieces once they start to brown.

5. Keeping the pan uncovered will allow coating to become crisp. For a softer coating, keep covered.

6. Once chicken is cooked through, serve with your favorite green veggies and enjoy!

MEATLESS MEATBALLS

(V, G, H, A) | SERVES 4-6

Ingredients

16 oz. spaghetti (use your favorite kind). Cook & set aside.

For the meatballs:

1 small onion, chopped

5 oz. crimini mushrooms, chopped (optional)

1 tsp. black pepper

1/4 tsp. salt

1 (15-oz.) cans black beans, drained

3 garlic cloves, chopped

2 Tbsp. Worcestershire sauce (V = use soy sauce or Bragg Liquid Aminos)

1/2 cup fresh parsley, chopped

1 cup oat bran (or buckwheat)

1/4 cup grated Parmesan or nutritional yeast

Directions

1. Preheat oven to 375 degrees and prepare a nonstick baking sheet by placing a piece of aluminum foil on it. Spread a thin layer of grapeseed oil over the foil with a paper towel.

2. Combine all ingredients in a blender or food processor and mix until a thick batter forms.

3. Form 2-inch meatballs with your hands and place on baking sheet. Bake for about 12 minutes, then flip the meatballs and bake another 10 minutes.

4. Add the meatballs to your favorite pasta and sauce!

5. (Hint: These go great with the Power Pasta recipe!)

6. Enjoy!

TURKEY MEATBALLS

(G, H, A) | SERVES 4-6

Note: This recipe is similar to the Meatless Meatballs, but here we use ground turkey instead of beans and we pan fry them in grapeseed oil.

Ingredients

16 oz. spaghetti (use your favorite kind). Cook and set aside.

For the meatballs:

4 Tbsp. grapeseed oil

1 small onion, chopped

5 oz. crimini mushrooms, chopped (optional)

1 tsp. black pepper

1/4 tsp. salt

1 lb. ground turkey

3 garlic cloves, chopped

2 Tbsp. Worcestershire sauce

1/2 cup fresh parsley, chopped

1 cup oat bran (or buckwheat)

1/4 cup grated Parmesan or nutritional yeast

Directions

1. Heat grapeseed oil in large skillet on a low heat.
2. Combine all ingredients in a large bowl and mix well to form a thick batter.
3. Form 2-inch meatballs with your hands and place in pan with oil.
4. Cook on all sides until outside is browned and inside is cooked through, about 10 minutes total. (Cut one open to be sure.)
5. Add the meatballs to your favorite pasta and sauce.
6. (Hint: These go great with the Power Pasta recipe!)
7. Enjoy!

STUFFED CABBAGE FLYTRAPS

(V, G, H, A) | SERVES 5-6

Ingredients

- 1/2 cup quinoa, cooked according to package directions
- 1 head of cabbage
- 1 small onion, diced
- 2-3 Tbsp. organic maple syrup
- 1/2 red pepper, diced
- 1/2 green pepper, diced
- large handful baby spinach
- 2 cloves garlic, minced
- 1 (15-oz.) can of red beans (or black beans), drained
- 2 (15-oz.) can diced tomatoes, drained
- sea salt, to taste
- black pepper, to taste
- 2 Tbsp. nutritional yeast (or Parmesan) (optional)
- 4 oz. crimini or Portabella mushrooms
- 3 Tbsp. grapeseed oil
- 4 tsp. dried basil

Directions

1. Preheat oven to 350 degrees.

2. Cook the quinoa before everything else so it's ready when you go to stuff the cabbage leaves, and set aside.

3. Sauté the onion, garlic and peppers in grapeseed oil on medium heat until tender.

4. Add in mushrooms and spinach and mix well. Cook another 2-3 minutes until mushrooms are browned and spinach is wilted.

5. Mix the beans, quinoa, salt, pepper and nutritional yeast (or Parmesan) into the onion mixture and stir well until everything is heated through, and set aside.

6. Now bring a large pot of water to a boil (big enough to fit the head of cabbage).

7. Core (cut out the center) of the cabbage and throw away. Place cabbage head in the boiling water. This will allow for easy stuffing of the leaves. Let boil about 2 minutes and remove from heat.

8. For the sauce: In a bowl, mix the tomatoes together with maple syrup and basil.

9. Add about 1/4 cup of the sauce to the quinoa mixture and mix.

10. Now remove the leaves and stuff each one with about 1/4 to 1/2 cup of the quinoa mixture depending on how large the cabbage leaf. Fold the cabbage leaf ends around the mixture and place seam-side down in a 9 x 12 casserole dish.

11. Pour remaining sauce over the cabbage rolls and cover. Bake for about 45-50 minutes.

12. Enjoy!

SMOKED VEGGIE PAELLA

(V, G, H, A) | SERVES 4-6

Note: The smoked paprika and turmeric are very important in this recipe.

Ingredients

- 5 cloves garlic, minced
- 7 oz. Portabella mushrooms, chopped
- 2 large bunches chard, leaves pulled from center stem & chopped
- 1 large yellow onion, chopped
- 5 whole artichoke hearts (canned in water is fine), cut into quarters
- 1 cup black rice, dry (a short grain brown rice, or quinoa works well, too)
- 4 1/2 cups low-sodium vegetable broth (keep some extra on the side)
- 4-5 vine-ripened tomatoes, seeded & diced
- 1 1/2 cups chickpeas, drained
- 3 Tbsp. grapeseed oil
- 1 Tbsp. smoked paprika
- 1 tsp. turmeric
- sea salt, to taste
- ground pepper, to taste

Directions

1. Drizzle extra large pan with grapeseed oil.

2. Sauté garlic and onions for about 5 minutes over medium heat until tender and then toss in the mushrooms and sauté until brown.

3. Add the uncooked rice to the pan and stir well.

4. Now add the tomatoes, chard, chickpeas, salt, pepper, turmeric and smoked paprika. Stir well for about a minute.

5. Pour in enough vegetable broth to cover the entire mixture and layer artichoke hearts on top. They'll eventually fall apart when you mix the paella later.

6. Reduce heat to a simmer and cover. Let cook about 40 minutes before uncovering and cooking another 15-20 minutes until rice is tender. As it cooks, you'll need to add more broth to the mixture so keep it at the ready!

7. Once it's done, set aside about 10-15 minutes and then serve.

QUINOA STUFFED PEPPERS

(G, H, A) | SERVES 4-6

Ingredients

4 Tbsp. grapeseed oil

1 15-oz. can black beans

1 celery stalk, chopped

1 sweet onion, chopped

3 cloves garlic, minced

7 oz. Portabella mushrooms, chopped

6 green, red & yellow bell peppers (two peppers of each color)

5 oz. baby spinach

3/4 tsp. ground cumin

1 cup uncooked quinoa, cooked according to package directions

sea salt, to taste

ground pepper, to taste

1/2 cup pecans, crushed

1 Tbsp. honey - or agave (V)

sprinkle of feta crumbles (optional)

Directions

1. Cook quinoa according to package directions and set aside.

2. Preheat oven to 350 degrees.

3. Using a paper towel, wipe a thin layer of grapeseed oil around a 9 x 12 casserole dish.

4. Slice peppers in half and remove the core and seeds. Lay peppers on their sides in casserole dish.

5. Next, heat grapeseed oil on low in large pan.

6. Add garlic, onion, celery and mushrooms. Cook about 8 minutes or until tender.

7. Add in spinach and allow to wilt. Then stir in cumin and cooked quinoa and mix well.

8. Now add salt, pepper and pecans and mix well for another minute.

9. Carefully stuff mixture into pepper halves and drizzle with honey. Cover with foil and bake 1 hour until peppers are soft.

10. Remove from oven and sprinkle with light layer of feta (optional).

11. Serve and enjoy!

PORTABELLA ASPARAGUS RISOTTO

(V, G, H, A) | SERVES 5

Ingredients

4-5 cups low-sodium vegetable broth (you may have leftover broth at the end)

1 lb. asparagus, tough bottoms removed

1 sweet onion, diced

4 Tbsp. grapeseed oil

1 1/2 cups Portabella or crimini mushrooms, chopped

1 stalk celery, minced

3 garlic cloves, minced

1 cup short grain brown rice

sea salt & freshly ground black pepper, to taste

1 1/2 cups sweet peas

small handful baby spinach

1/3 cup nutritional yeast flakes (or Parmesan)

1/4 cup freshly chopped parsley

1 tsp. lemon zest (grated lemon peel)

PORTABELLA ASPARAGUS RISOTTO

Directions

1. Note: This whole process takes a little over an hour.

2. In a pan, sauté onion, celery, garlic and asparagus in grapeseed oil on medium heat for about 5 minutes. Add the mushrooms and cook another 2-3 minutes until tender.

3. Now add the dry rice to the mixture and stir well for about 4 minutes.

4. Add 1/2 cup of broth. Sprinkle in salt and pepper and stir well.

5. Now reduce the heat and let mixture absorb the broth before adding another 1/2 cup of broth.

6. Repeat this process of adding 1/2 cup of broth 4 times (or as many times as it takes to soften rice). Let the mixture absorb the broth each time before adding more.

7. Finally, add in the sweet peas, spinach, parsley and lemon zest. Cook another 10 minutes, mixing constantly.

8. Rice should be tender at this point and risotto should have a creamy consistency.

9. Serve and enjoy!

DATES & CASHEW QUINOA SALAD

(V, G, H, A) | SERVES 2

Ingredients

2-3 large handfuls baby spinach

1/2 cup cooked quinoa

1/2 cup whole cashews, crushed

1/2 cup dates, pitted & minced

sprinkle of feta cheese crumbles (optional)

Directions

1. Combine all ingredients except feta in large bowl and mix.

2. Divide salad into two bowls.

3. Add optional Honey Vinaigrette Dressing (next page) and sprinkle with feta.

HONEY VINAIGRETTE

(G, H, A) | SERVES 2

Ingredients

2 Tbsp. honey

4 Tbsp. extra virgin olive oil

1 Tbsp. apple cider vinegar

1 Tbsp. water

Directions

Whisk honey, olive oil, vinegar and water in bowl until well combined and drizzle over salads.

NOODLES A LA ROON

(V, G, H, A) | SERVES 2-4

Note: Feel free to experiment by adding in ingredients like spinach, onions and mushrooms before baking.

Ingredients

16 oz. of your favorite whole wheat or gluten-free pasta noodle

16 oz. plain 2% cottage cheese - or blend silken tofu with a dash of lemon juice (V)

1/2 lb. ground turkey (optional)

sea salt, to taste

black pepper, to taste

1/4 cup nutritional yeast or Parmesan

PHOTO: CHRISTINE ASHTON

Directions

1. Preheat oven to 350 degrees.
2. Boil noodles until soft, rinse and drain and add to a large casserole dish.
3. If using turkey meat, brown in pan and drain juices. Add to casserole dish.
4. Add cottage cheese to casserole dish along with salt and pepper. Mix well.
5. Sprinkle top of casserole with nutritional yeast or Parmesan and bake for 20-30 minutes until the tips of the noodles at the top of the casserole brown.
6. Serve and enjoy!

SWEET CITRUS SPINACH SALAD

(V, G, H, A) | SERVES 2-4

Ingredients

5 oz. (or 2 large handfuls) baby spinach

1/2 cucumber, peeled & sliced into rounds

5-6 mandarin oranges, peeled & divided

1/2 cup pine nuts

1/4 cup apple cider vinegar

1/2 cup extra virgin olive oil

1 Tbsp. agave & drizzle of agave for pine nuts

dash of black pepper

Directions

1. Divide spinach, cucumber and mandarin oranges among serving bowls.

2. Add pine nuts to small pan and lightly drizzle with agave. Toast pine nuts for about 1-2 minutes, stirring constantly. Set aside when done.

3. Whisk together apple cider vinegar, olive oil, 1 Tbsp. agave and black pepper in a small bowl and drizzle over salad. Add pine nuts to the tops of each salad.

SEARED AHI TUNA STEAKS

(G, H, A) | SERVES 2-4

Ingredients

1 lb. sashimi grade yellow fin tuna, cut into serving portions

sea salt, to taste

black pepper, to taste

1/2 cup oat bran or buckwheat

1 Tbsp. Italian seasoning

3 Tbsp. grapeseed oil

Directions

1. Roll the tuna in the oat bran or buckwheat and the sprinkle with salt, pepper and Italian seasoning.
2. Drizzle grapeseed oil in large pan and put on high heat.
3. Place the tuna in the pan, searing it on all sides (about 30-40 seconds per side).
4. Remove from pan and plate.
5. Pair with your favorite sides or put on top of leafy green salad and enjoy!

CINNAMON ORANGE PECAN CHICKEN

(G, H, A) | SERVES 4-6

Ingredients

4 skinless, boneless chicken breasts, each sliced in half lengthwise

4 Tbsp. organic maple syrup

1 cup pecans, crushed

3 Tbsp. grapeseed oil

dash of sea salt

dash of black pepper

3 oranges, 2 sliced into wedges & 1 juiced (if you don't own a juicer, just squeeze it!)

1 tsp. ground cumin

1/2 tsp. cayenne pepper

1 Tbsp. cinnamon

Directions

1. Trim any fatty parts from chicken breasts.

2. Place maple syrup in bowl and crushed pecans in another.

3. Roll chicken in 2 Tbsp. maple syrup and then in the crushed pecans.

4. Drizzle 3 Tbsp. grapeseed oil in pan and turn on medium heat.

5. Sprinkle chicken with salt and pepper and place in pan.

6. Drizzle with 1 Tbsp. syrup and press the rest of the pecans from the bowl onto the chicken breasts.

7. Cook about 4 minutes on each side until cooked through.

8. In a small pan, add orange juice, 1 Tbsp. syrup, cayenne and cumin.

9. Cook uncovered about 1-2 minutes until thickened.

10. Put chicken on serving plates and pour orange mixture over chicken.

11. Sprinkle with a pinch of cinnamon and serve with orange wedges.

PEACH-GLAZED TURKEY BREAST

(G, H, A) | SERVES 4-6

Ingredients

4 boneless, skinless turkey breasts, each sliced in half lengthwise

3-4 peaches, sliced

2 Tbsp. agave

2 cloves garlic, minced

dash of sea salt

dash of black pepper

Directions

1. Preheat oven to 350 degrees.

2. Using small pan, sauté minced garlic in grapeseed oil for about 2 minutes and set aside.

3. Place turkey breasts in baking dish and place peach halves around them.

4. Drizzle turkey with agave and sprinkle with sautéed garlic, sea salt and pepper.

5. Bake about 45 minutes until turkey is done throughout.

TANGY BEET & SPINACH SALAD

(V, G, H, A)   SERVES 2-4

Ingredients

6 beets

1 Tbsp. grapeseed oil

3 Tbsp. extra virgin olive oil

1 Tbsp. apple cider vinegar

4-5 oz. baby spinach

1/2 cup pecans roughly chopped & toasted

2 oz. goat cheese or feta (optional)

dash of black pepper

Directions:

1. Preheat oven to 450 degrees.

2. Preparing beets: Trim stems and root. Wash and pat dry. Place in baking dish, brush with grapeseed oil and cover tightly with 2 layers of aluminum foil. Bake for 1 hour. Beets should be tender when done. Allow to cool to room temperature before scraping off beet skin with paring knife. Cut beets into bite-sized pieces.

3. Add beets to a large bowl along with spinach and pecans and mix well. Separate into serving bowls.

4. In another small bowl, blend olive oil, apple cider vinegar and a little black pepper. Drizzle over each salad. Top with goat cheese or feta.

5. Enjoy!

APPLE PECAN SALAD

(V, G, H, A) | SERVES 2-4

Ingredients

2 large handfuls baby spinach

2 handfuls arugula

1/2 cup alfalfa sprouts

1 apple, chopped

1/2 cup chickpeas

2 Tbsp. chopped pecans

2 Tbsp. dried cranberries

Dressing:

4 Tbsp. extra virgin olive oil

2 Tbsp. apple cider vinegar

dash of black pepper

Directions

1. In a small bowl, whisk together apple cider vinegar and olive oil with a dash of black pepper.

2. In a large bowl, combine everything else.

3. Separate portions in serving bowls and drizzle with dressing.

4. Enjoy!

MOM'S MEATLOAF IN A PINCH

(G, H, A) | SERVES 4-6

Ingredients

- **1 lb. ground turkey**
- **2 eggs**
- **1 small onion, minced**
- **2 garlic cloves, minced**
- **1/2 cup oat bran (or buckwheat)**
- **2 Tbsp. maple syrup**
- **1 Tbsp. Worcestershire sauce**
- **dash of sea salt**
- **1 Tbsp. grapeseed oil**

Directions

1. Preheat oven to 350 degrees.
2. In a large bowl, combine all ingredients and mix well.
3. Wipe grapeseed oil on inside of loaf pan and transfer mixture to the pan.
4. Bake for 45 minutes.
5. Remove from oven, slice and serve with your favorite sides.

CHICKEN & ASPARAGUS STIR-FRY

(G, H, A) | SERVES 2-4

Ingredients

2 chicken breasts cut into bite-sized pieces

1 bunch thin asparagus (about 20 stalks)

2 cloves garlic, chopped

1 medium shallot, minced

2 Tbsp. low-sodium soy sauce or teriyaki sauce

Directions

1. Cut off thick ends of asparagus; wash what remains and cut into bite-sized pieces.

2. Steam for about 7-10 minutes, or until bright green, and then set aside.

3. In a large pan, sauté shallot and garlic in peanut oil for about 2 minutes.

4. Add chicken and continue to sauté about 6 minutes or until pink disappears.

5. Pour into heat-safe serving bowl and mix in asparagus.

6. Add 2 Tbsp. low-sodium soy sauce or teriyaki sauce and serve.

TURKEY BURGERS

(G, H, A) | SERVES 2

Ingredients

1/2 lb. lean turkey

1/4 cup oat bran or buckwheat (G)

1 whole egg

2 cloves garlic, chopped

1 tsp. Worcestershire or teriyaki sauce

dash each of sea salt, pepper & oregano

Optional toppings:

Romaine lettuce

sliced tomato

dill pickle

avocado

cheese

ketchup

mustard

Directions

1. Lightly coat pan with grapeseed oil and set on low-medium heat.
2. In a large bowl, combine everything except toppings and mix well.
3. Shape into 4 to 5 palm-sized patties.
4. Place patties in pan and flatten with spatula.
5. Grill, covered, over indirect medium heat for 4-6 minutes on each side or until meat is no longer pink inside.
6. Serve on bread or wrapped in lettuce with optional toppings.

FIGHTER FAJITAS

(V, G, H, A) | SERVES 4-6

Ingredients

> **1 lb. skinless, boneless chicken breasts (optional, not Vegan)**
>
> **16 oz. black beans (V)**
>
> **1 tsp. chili powder**
>
> **1/2 tsp. sea salt**
>
> **1/2 tsp. ground cumin**
>
> **1/2 tsp. freshly ground black pepper**
>
> **8-12 whole wheat or gluten-free tortillas**

For toppings:

> **1 avocado, mashed in bowl with 1 Tbsp. lemon juice. Set aside.**
>
> **1 chopped tomato**
>
> **1/4 head of lettuce, chopped**
>
> **shredded cheddar cheese (optional)**

Directions

1. Preheat oven to 350 degrees.
2. Coat pan in grapeseed oil and set on low-medium heat.
3. Combine chili powder, sea salt, cumin and black pepper in a small bowl.
4. Chop raw chicken in bite-sized pieces and sprinkle with spices.
5. Place chicken in pan and cook 10 minutes, stirring often, until done.
6. Heat tortillas on cookie sheet in oven for 2 minutes and remove.
7. Divide chicken evenly among tortillas; top each tortilla with a sprinkle of lettuce, tomato, avocado and cheese.

HONEY-GLAZED SALMON

(G, H, A) | SERVES 1

Ingredients

8 oz. wild-caught salmon

dash of sea salt

1 Tbsp. honey or agave

Directions

1. Coat small pan with grapeseed oil and put on low-medium heat.
2. Rub salmon with grapeseed oil and sprinkle with sea salt.
3. Cook 3-5 minutes on each side, depending on thickness.
4. Salmon should be cooked evenly through the center.
5. Plate and drizzle with honey or agave.

POWER PASTA SAUCE

(V, G, H, A) | SERVES 4-6

This sauce makes a great dip for bread, serve it over pasta or chicken, or mix with rice or quinoa for a hearty meal.

Ingredients

16 oz. pasta (whole wheat, durum, brown rice, quinoa or gluten-free pasta noodles)

4 16-oz. cans of diced tomatoes or 12-14 whole tomatoes, steamed, peeled & crushed

1 red pepper, chopped

1 green pepper, chopped

1 medium sweet onion, chopped

10-12 cloves garlic, diced

1 pinch each of basil, oregano & sea salt

16 oz. organic ground turkey (optional - not vegan)

extra virgin olive oil

grapeseed oil

Directions

1. Pour diced tomatoes in large pot and heat over low-medium flame.

2. Add basil, oregano and sea salt before covering to simmer.

3. Sauté garlic, onion and peppers in grapeseed oil over low-medium heat.

4. In another pan at low-medium heat, begin to brown the turkey in grapeseed oil.

5. In another large pot, bring 6-8 cups water to boil.

6. Once vegetables have softened to your taste, add to sauce.

7. When turkey has thoroughly cooked, add to sauce, cover and simmer another 10 minutes before removing from heat.

8. Add pasta noodles to boiling water and cook for 8-12 minutes.

9. Stir in 2 Tbsp. extra virgin olive oil.

10. When noodles are done, add separately to plates and cover with sauce.

GARLIC PORTABELLA CHICKEN WITH ASPARAGUS & SPINACH

(V, G, H, A) | SERVES 1-2

Ingredients

1/2 chicken breast, cut into bite-sized pieces – or eliminate chicken & use whole Portabella mushroom top (V)

1/3 Portabella mushroom, chopped

handful baby spinach

1 Tbsp. garlic, minced

half bunch asparagus (6-8 stalks), steamed

dash each of sea salt, oregano & pepper

Directions

1. Coat medium pan with grapeseed oil and put on low-medium heat.
2. Add Portabella mushroom and garlic to pan.
3. Once mushrooms brown, add handful of spinach leaves and sauté until spinach shrinks into mushroom mixture.
4. Add asparagus.
5. In separate pan, sprinkle chicken with spices and sauté in grapeseed oil.
6. Once cooked, add chicken to mushroom pan. Lightly stir mixture.
7. Let cook together for 5 minutes, then plate.

SKINNY SUMO STIR-FRY

(V, G, H, A) | SERVES 1-2

Ingredients

1 chicken breast, cut into bite-sized pieces – or serve over quinoa instead (V)

2 cups broccoli, chopped

1 cup mushrooms, chopped

1 Tbsp. low-sodium soy sauce or 2 sprays of Bragg Liquid Aminos

4 green onions, chopped

handful bean sprouts

Directions

1. Coat small pan with peanut oil and cook chicken until no longer pink inside.
2. Steam broccoli in separate pan until tender.
3. In another pan, sauté mushrooms in peanut oil until browned.
4. Combine chicken, mushrooms and broccoli in bowl.
5. Top with onions, sprouts and low-sodium soy sauce.

BAKED CHICKEN DINNER

(G, H, A) | SERVES 1-2

Ingredients

1 chicken breast, sliced in half lengthwise

dash of sea salt

dash of pepper

Directions

1. Preheat oven to 350 degrees.
2. Rub chicken with grapeseed oil and sprinkle with sea salt and pepper. Place in baking dish and cook for 20 minutes or until no longer pink inside.

SPINACH PASTA

(V, G, H, A) | SERVES 4-6

Ingredients

16 oz. whole wheat or brown rice noodles, or 1 cup quinoa

handful fresh baby spinach

1 cup basil leaves, tightly packed

3 cloves garlic, minced

1 Tbsp. grapeseed oil

1/3 cup almond milk

1/2 cup mozzarella cheese, shredded (optional – not vegan)

sea salt & pepper to taste

SHOWN TOPPED WITH
SUN-DRIED TOMATOES.

PHOTO: CHRISTINE ASHTON

Directions

1. Cook pasta according to package directions.

2. Chop spinach and basil in blender or food processor. If you don't have a chopping appliance, just shred by hand.

3. In a large saucepan, sauté garlic in grapeseed oil.

4. Add milk and spinach mixture to saucepan. Bring to a boil, then reduce heat to a simmer. Stir occasionally until sauce slightly thickens and remove from heat.

5. Drain water and add noodles to spinach mixture in saucepan. Add cheese, sea salt and pepper. Serve immediately.

CHAMPION CHILI

(V, G, H, A) | SERVES 4-6

Ingredients

1/2 lb. ground organic turkey - or 1 can chickpeas (V)

2 cans diced tomatoes or 6-7 freshly chopped tomatoes

1 can kidney beans

1 red pepper, chopped

1 green pepper, chopped

1 sweet onion, chopped

4 cloves garlic, chopped

sea salt, to taste

chili powder, to taste

1 cup shredded rice cheddar cheese (optional)

PHOTO: CHRISTINE ASHTON

Directions

1. Put tomatoes and beans in large pot and place on low heat.
2. Brown meat in separate pan and add to tomato pot.
3. In another pan, sauté peppers, onions and garlic in grapeseed oil. Once tender, add to tomato pot.
4. Add sea salt and chili powder to taste.
5. Sprinkle with cheese and serve.

COD OR TILAPIA

(G, H, A) | SERVES 1

Ingredients

1 cod or tilapia filet

1 dash each of sea salt, rosemary & pepper

1/2 lemon, juiced

Directions

1. Heat oven to 350 degrees.
2. Rub fish with grapeseed oil and spices.
3. Bake in casserole dish for 15 minutes.
4. Squeeze fresh lemon juice over filet and serve.

THORO-BREADED "FRIED" CHICKEN

(G, H, A)   SERVES 1-2

Ingredients

1 chicken breast, sliced horizontally

1 cup oat bran or buckwheat (G)

1 egg

1/3 cup almond milk

1 Tbsp. ground flax seeds

Directions

1. Mix 1 egg and 1/3 cup milk in small bowl.

2. Combine oat bran and flax seeds in separate bowl.

3. Coat pan with coconut oil and heat over low-medium flame.

4. Dip chicken in egg/milk mixture, and then roll chicken in oat bran/flax seeds mixture to coat.

5. Immediately place in pan. Cook 3-4 minutes on each side.

PINEAPPLE CHICKEN "FRIED" QUINOA

(V, G, H, A) | SERVES 3-4

Ingredients

1 cup uncooked quinoa

1 organic chicken breast, cut into bite-sized pieces – or use tofu, extra firm, cubed (V)

1 cup crushed pineapple

2 eggs, beaten (optional)

3/4 cup mushrooms, chopped

3 Tbsp. low-sodium soy sauce or Bragg Liquid Aminos

3 green onions, thinly sliced

1 cup carrots, diced

Directions

1. Add 1 cup quinoa and 2 cups water to large saucepan.
2. Bring to boil, reduce heat and cover for 15 minutes.
3. Coat small pan with coconut oil and cook chicken.
4. (Skip next two steps if making Vegan option)
5. Coat another small pan with coconut oil and cook eggs without stirring.
6. Once solid, put eggs on cutting surface and chop.
7. Using egg pan, sauté mushrooms, green onions and carrots until tender.
8. Stir in quinoa, pineapple and egg pieces.
9. Add chicken to vegetable mixture.
10. Add soy sauce or spray with Bragg Liquid Aminos and stir. Serve hot.

SIDES & SNACKS

ROSEMARY & THYME ASPARAGUS

(V, G, H, A) | SERVES 4

Ingredients

1 sweet onion, chopped

4 oz. crimini mushrooms, sliced

2 Tbsp. grapeseed oil

1 lb. fresh green beans, ends trimmed

2 tsp. fresh rosemary

1 tsp. fresh thyme

1 clove garlic, minced

dash of sea salt

dash of pepper

Directions

1. Sauté onions, green beans and garlic in grapeseed oil about 5 minutes.

2. Add mushrooms, rosemary and thyme, salt and pepper and heat for about 5 more minutes, stirring often.

3. Cover and cook another 5-8 minutes until beans are tender.

4. Serve and enjoy!

MASHED SWEET POTATOES

(V, G, H, A) | SERVES 2-3

Ingredients

2 large sweet potatoes

3 Tbsp. almond milk

2 Tbsp. plain Greek yogurt or soy yogurt (V) (both optional)

2 Tbsp. agave

dash of cinnamon

dash of sea salt

Directions

1. Wash and peel potatoes and cut into hunks.

2. Boil large pot of water and add potatoes. Cook about 20-30 minutes until a fork easily goes through them.

3. Drain water.

4. Mash potatoes in the pot and add the rest of the ingredients, mixing well. If you have an electric beater, you can use that to make them extra creamy, but a fork or potato masher will do just fine.

5. Serve and enjoy!

SWEET POTATO FRIES

(V, G, H, A) | SERVES 2-3

Ingredients

2 large sweet potatoes

3 Tbsp. agave (or honey)

dash of sea salt

2 Tbsp. grapeseed oil

Directions

1. Preheat oven to 375 degrees.
2. Wash and peel potatoes and cut into thin, French-fry-like strips.
3. In large bowl, combine 1 Tbsp. grapeseed oil and salt.
4. Toss sweet potatoes in mixture.
5. Spread 1 Tbsp. grapeseed oil over baking sheet and spread out potatoes in single layer.
6. Bake about 30 minutes or until tender on the inside and crispy on the outside.
7. Transfer to serving plate. Add honey to small bowl for dipping.
8. Enjoy!

SAUTÉED MUSHROOM & GARLIC STRING BEANS

(V, G, H, A) | SERVES 5-6

Ingredients

2 lbs. fresh (or frozen) organic green beans

9 large shiitake mushrooms (fresh, not dried)

4-5 medium cloves of garlic, minced

Directions

1. Wash beans, cut off ends, and snap them in half.
2. Steam the green beans until tender. Drain and set aside.
3. Coat large pan with grapeseed oil and place on low-medium heat.
4. Add garlic and mushrooms and cook for 3 minutes, stirring occasionally.
5. Mix in the green beans and sauté for 6-8 minutes, until beans are browned.
6. Serve with quinoa, fish or chicken.

EASY BAKED BEANS

(V, G, H, A)　|　SERVES 2-3

Ingredients

15 oz. cannellini beans, drained & rinsed

3 Tbsp. ketchup

2 Tbsp. Dijon mustard

3 Tbsp. organic maple syrup

1 tsp. smoked paprika

Directions

1. Preheat oven to 350 degrees.
2. Combine all ingredients together and bake in casserole dish 30 minutes or until bubbling.

CANDIED BABY CARROTS

(V, G, H, A) | SERVES 2-3

Ingredients

2 cups organic baby carrots

1/2 cup orange juice (fresh squeezed if possible)

1 cup water

1 tsp. maple syrup or agave (optional)

Directions

1. Boil water and orange juice together in a small pot and add in carrots.

2. Cook about 10 minutes or until carrots are tender.

3. Drain carrots and serve. (You can also drizzle with maple syrup or agave before serving.)

MUSCLE SPROUTS

(V, G, H, A) | SERVES 2-4

Ingredients

14-20 Brussels sprouts, halved

4 Tbsp. grapeseed oil

4-5 sprays of Bragg's Liquid Aminos, or a tsp. of low-sodium soy sauce

Directions

1. Heat grapeseed oil in large pan over medium heat.

2. Add Brussels sprouts, flat sides down and cook until browned, then flip and brown other side.

3. Transfer Brussels sprouts to serving dish and spray with Bragg's (or soy sauce).

ZUCCHINI IN RED SAUCE

(V, G, H, A) | SERVES 2-4

Ingredients

2 zucchinis, peeled & sliced

2 Tbsp. grapeseed oil

1 15-oz. can diced tomatoes

dash of sea salt

dash of pepper

Directions

1. In a small pan, sauté zucchini in grapeseed oil until tender and then add diced tomatoes and gently stir.

2. Add salt and pepper and serve.

GARLIC SNOW PEAS

(V, G, H, A) | SERVES 1-2

Ingredients

2 cups fresh snow peas

1 Tbsp. toasted sesame seeds

2 minced garlic cloves

2 Tbsp. grapeseed oil

dash of sea salt

dash of black pepper

Directions

1. In medium pan, sauté snow peas in grapeseed oil about 5 minutes or until bright green.

2. Add in garlic, sesame seeds, and salt and pepper.

3. Serve and enjoy!

BAKED AVOCADO FRIES

(V, G, H, A) | SERVES 2-4

Ingredients

2 avocados, peeled & sliced

Add a pinch of the following spices in a small bowl & blend:

sea salt

black pepper

onion powder

turmeric (optional)

chili (or cayenne powder)

PHOTO: CHRISTINE ASHTON

Directions

1. Preheat oven to 375 degrees.

2. Put avocados on a baking tray lined with foil.

3. Sprinkle the seasoning over the avocado slices.

4. Put the trays into the oven and bake for 10 minutes.

5. Remove from oven and flip each one carefully. Add some seasoning to the naked sides of the avocados and bake for about 20 minutes or until outsides get a bit crispy.

6. When they're done, sprinkle a little more seasoning on them, to taste.

7. Serve alone, as a snack or as a side.

VEGGIE TRAY WITH DOLCE MINT TZATZIKI DIP

(G, H, A) | SERVES 2-4

Ingredients

Vegetable: Broccoli, small carrots, cherry tomatoes, celery slices or your favorites! (Option: This dip also goes well with pita chips.)

For Dip:

2 (8-oz.) containers plain Greek yogurt - or soy yogurt (V)

2 cucumbers, diced small

1 Tbsp. olive oil

1/2 lemon, juiced

sea salt & pepper (to taste)

1 Tbsp. chopped fresh mint leaves

3 cloves garlic, chopped small

Directions

Wash vegetables, then chop and set aside.

For Dip:

1. Combine all ingredients well.
2. Cover and refrigerate for at least 1 hour.
3. Serve cold with veggies or pita chips!

SPINACH STUFFED MUSHROOMS

(V, G, H, A) | SERVES 2-4

Ingredients

8-oz. package of white button mushrooms

3 large cloves of garlic, minced

4 cups of baby spinach leaves, chopped (hard stems removed)

2 Tbsp. nutritional yeast or Parmesan, shredded

sea salt & pepper

2 Tbsp. grapeseed oil

Directions

1. Preheat oven to 400 degrees.

2. Wash mushrooms. Remove and mince the stems. Set stems aside.

3. Heat grapeseed oil in medium pan and add garlic and mushroom stems. Sauté about 3-5 minutes and add spinach. Cook until wilted. Add salt and pepper, mix well and remove from heat.

4. Line up mushrooms on baking sheet and stuff them with the spinach mixture.

5. Sprinkle with nutritional yeast or Parmesan cheese and bake for about 20 minutes.

6. Serve hot.

FRESH SALSA

(V, G, H, A) | SERVES 2-4

Ingredients

3 medium tomatoes, chopped

1/2 red onion, finely diced

2 small cloves of garlic, minced

1 lime, juiced

1/2 cup chopped cilantro

salt & pepper to taste

few sprinkles of oregano

1 jalapeño chili pepper, diced (optional)

Directions

1. Combine all of the ingredients in a bowl.

2. Taste, and season to your liking.

3. Refrigerate for an hour and serve with your favorite sea-salted pita chips or homemade tortilla chips - recipes for these are in this book!

STRAWBERRY AVOCADO SALSA

(V, G, H, A)   SERVES 2-4

Ingredients

> **2 cups fresh strawberries, diced**
>
> **1 jalapeño, finely chopped**
>
> **1 avocado, diced**
>
> **1/4 cup red onion, diced**
>
> **fresh cilantro**
>
> **splash of lime juice**

Directions

> Marinate 30 minutes and serve with your favorite organic chips.

HOMEBAKED TORTILLA CHIPS

(V, G, H, A) | SERVES 2-4

Ingredients

gluten-free tortillas cut into triangles

1 Tbsp. grapeseed oil

dash of sea salt

Directions

1. Preheat oven to 350 degrees.
2. Place tortilla pieces on baking sheet and brush with grapeseed oil.
3. Sprinkle with salt.
4. Bake about 8 minutes until crisp.
5. Serve and enjoy!

SMOKEY TORTILLA CHIPS

(V, G, H, A) | SERVES 2-4

Ingredients

gluten-free tortillas, cut into triangles

1 Tbsp. grapeseed oil

dash of smoked paprika

dash of sea salt

Directions

1. Preheat oven to 350 degrees.
2. Place tortilla pieces on baking sheet and brush with grapeseed oil.
3. Sprinkle with salt and smoked paprika.
4. Bake about 8 minutes until crisp.
5. Serve and enjoy!

ITALIAN TORTILLA CHIPS

(V, G, H, A) | SERVES 2-4

Ingredients

gluten-free tortillas, cut into triangles

1 Tbsp. grapeseed oil

dash of Italian seasoning

sprinkle of Parmesan or nutritional yeast (V)

dash of sea salt

Directions

1. Preheat oven to 350 degrees.
2. Place tortilla pieces on baking sheet and brush with grapeseed oil.
3. Sprinkle with salt, Italian seasoning and Parmesan (or nutritional yeast).
4. Bake about 8 minutes until crisp.
5. Serve and enjoy!

GRAM'S BAKED APPLES

(V, G, H, A)   SERVES 2-4

Ingredients

4 large apples

3/4 cup plain almond milk

sprinkle of Saigon cinnamon

sprinkle of nutmeg

drizzle of organic maple syrup

1/2 cup golden raisins

Directions

1. Preheat oven to 375 degrees.

2. Slice apples in half. Clean out the seeds and hard center. Place in baking dish.

3. Coat in maple syrup and then almond milk.

4. Add in raisins.

5. Sprinkle with cinnamon and nutmeg.

6. Bake 40 minutes while intermittently basting apples with the milk/syrup mixture from bottom of baking dish. The apples are done when a fork easily pierces the apple.

7. Remove from oven and let cool about 10 minutes.

8. Place apples in bowls and spoon the almond/maple syrup mixture over the apples again in the bowls. Be sure to get the raisins, too!

9. You can always add more almond milk/syrup to taste.

10. Enjoy!

ROASTED CHICKPEAS

(V, G, H, A) | SERVES 2-4

Ingredients

1 can (14 oz.) chickpeas, drained

1 Tbsp. grapeseed oil

1 tsp. cinnamon

1 tsp. nutmeg

2 Tbsp. maple syrup

dash of sea salt

PHOTO: CHRISTINE ASHTON

Directions

1. Preheat oven to 450 degrees.

2. Spread chickpeas on baking sheet and bake for about 40 minutes.

3. Put rest of ingredients in large bowl.

4. When chickpeas are done cooking, transfer them to the bowl and coat with the remaining ingredients.

5. Enjoy!

HENRIETTA'S BRUSCHETTA
(Who's Henrietta?)

(V, G, H, A) | SERVES 2-4

Ingredients

4 vine-ripened tomatoes, seeded & diced

1/2 red pepper, diced

2 cloves garlic, minced

1 tsp. grapeseed oil

1 Tbsp. extra virgin olive oil

1 tsp. balsamic vinegar

1/4 cup fresh basil, minced

sea salt, to taste

pepper, to taste

1/4 cup fresh mozzarella, shredded (optional)

whole wheat or gluten-free baguette, sliced

Directions

1. Preheat oven to 350 degrees.

2. Combine red pepper, tomatoes, basil, sea salt, pepper, mozzarella and garlic in bowl and toss with olive oil. Refrigerate about 30 minutes until chilled.

3. Meanwhile, slice bread and place on baking sheet. Brush with grapeseed oil and bake 5-8 minutes until lightly toasted.

4. Top with tomato mixture and serve immediately.

KIWI MANGO CHIA PUDDING

(V, G, H, A) | SERVES 1

Ingredients

1/4 cup chia seed

1/4 cup water

1/2 mango, diced

1 kiwi, diced

1 tsp. agave

Directions

1. Combine chia seed and water in small bowl and let sit for about an hour until thick and pudding-like.

2. Top with kiwi and mango.

3. Drizzle with agave and serve.

BLUEBERRY MADNESS

(G, H, A) | SERVES 1

Ingredients

- **6 oz. plain Greek yogurt**
- **1/2 cup blueberries**
- **1 Tbsp. agave or honey**
- **1 tsp. chia seed**

Directions

Combine all ingredients in bowl and enjoy!

CHERRY & NUT GO BARS

(G, H, A) | SERVES 3

Ingredients

1/2 cup chopped dates (try to get from your produce section - if you have to get pre-packaged dates, wash them in warm water before using to help get rid of any preservative)

1/2 cup cherries, pitted & chopped

1/2 cup pecans

1/2 tsp. cinnamon

1 tsp. maple syrup (optional)

1 tsp. ground flaxseed

Directions

1. First, lay out three 12 x 12 pieces of plastic wrap.
2. Next, put dates and cherries in your food processor or blender and blend until a paste forms. Put in bowl and set aside.
3. Now add the nuts to the blender and chop them up.
4. Add the nuts, cinnamon, flaxseed and syrup to the bowl with the cherries and with a wooden spoon (or your fingers) mush the mixture together until well blended.
5. Divide the mixture into thirds and place in each of the three pieces of plastic wrap laid out earlier and wrap up the mixture tightly.
6. Shape the mixture into bars (a rolling pin helps) and keep wrapped.
7. Refrigerate for about an hour and they're ready to eat!

CRANBERRY, RAISIN & PEANUT GO BARS

(G, H, A) | SERVES 3

Ingredients

1/2 cup raisins

1/2 cup dried cranberries

1/2 cup peanuts, unsalted

1 tsp. maple syrup (optional)

1 tsp. ground flaxseed

Directions

1. First, lay out three 12 x 12 pieces of plastic wrap.

2. Next, put raisins and cranberries in your food processor or blender and blend until a paste forms. Put in bowl and set aside.

3. Now add the nuts to the blender and chop them up.

4. Add the nuts, flaxseed and syrup to the bowl with the raisins and with a wooden spoon (or your fingers) mush the mixture together until well blended.

5. Divide the mixture into thirds and place in each of the three pieces of plastic wrap laid out earlier and wrap up the mixture tightly.

6. Shape the mixture into bars (a rolling pin helps) and keep wrapped.

7. Refrigerate for about an hour and they're ready to eat!

APRICOT & NUT GO BARS

(G, H, A) | SERVES 3

Ingredients

3/4 cup apricots

1/4 cup dates, chopped

1/4 cup pecans

1/4 cup walnuts

1/2 tsp. cinnamon

1 tsp. maple syrup (optional)

1 tsp. ground flaxseed

Directions

1. First, lay out three 12 x 12 pieces of plastic wrap.

2. Next, put apricots and dates in your food processor or blender and blend until a paste forms. Put in bowl and set aside.

3. Now add the nuts to the blender and chop them up.

4. Add the nuts, cinnamon, flaxseed and syrup to the bowl with the apricot mixture and with a wooden spoon (or your fingers) mush the mixture together until well blended.

5. Divide the mixture into thirds and place in each of the three pieces of plastic wrap laid out earlier and wrap up the mixture tightly.

6. Shape the mixture into bars (a rolling pin helps) and keep wrapped.

7. Refrigerate for about an hour and they're ready to eat!

APPLE & HONEY GO BARS

(G, H, A) | SERVES 3

Ingredients

- **1 apple**
- **1 cup dates**
- **1/4 cup pecans**
- **1 tsp. cinnamon**
- **1 tsp. nutmeg**
- **1 Tbsp. honey (optional)**
- **1/4 cup ground flaxseed**

Directions

1. First, lay out three 12 x 12 pieces of plastic wrap.
2. Next, put apples and dates in your food processor or blender and blend until a paste forms. Put in bowl and set aside.
3. Now add the pecans to the blender and chop them up.
4. Add the nuts, cinnamon, nutmeg, flaxseed and honey to the bowl with the apple mixture and with a wooden spoon (or your fingers) mush the mixture together until well blended.
5. Divide the mixture into thirds and place in each of the three pieces of plastic wrap laid out earlier and wrap up the mixture tightly.
6. Shape the mixture into bars (a rolling pin helps) and keep wrapped.
7. Refrigerate for about an hour and they're ready to eat!

BLUEBERRY & DATE GO BARS

(G, H, A) | SERVES 3

Ingredients

1 1/2 cups fresh blueberries

1 tsp. fresh lemon juice

1/2 tsp. lemon zest

1 cup dates

1/4 cup pecans

1 tsp. cinnamon

1 Tbsp. honey (optional)

1/4 cup ground flaxseed

Directions

1. First, lay out three 12 x 12 pieces of plastic wrap.

2. Next, put all ingredients except the blueberries in a food processor or blender and blend until a paste forms. Put paste in bowl and add blueberries.

3. With a wooden spoon (or your fingers) mush the mixture together until well blended.

4. Divide the mixture into thirds and place in each of the three pieces of plastic wrap laid out earlier and wrap up the mixture tightly.

5. Shape the mixture into bars (a rolling pin helps) and keep wrapped.

6. Refrigerate for about an hour and they're ready to eat!

SMOOTHIES

BLUEBERRY BANANA SMOOTHIE

(V, G, H, A) | SERVES 1-2

Ingredients

1 cup blueberries

1 banana

2 dates

1 cup water

1/2 cup ice

1 Tbsp. ground flaxseed

1 Tbsp. hemp oil

1 tsp. agave

Directions

Blend together and enjoy!

KIWI MANGO SMOOTHIE

(V, G, H, A) | SERVES 1-2

Ingredients

- **1 cup fresh mango**
- **1 cup fresh kiwi**
- **1/4 cup buckwheat**
- **handful baby spinach**
- **1 cup water**
- **1/2 cup ice**
- **1 Tbsp. ground flaxseed**
- **1 Tbsp. hemp oil**
- **1 tsp. agave**

Directions

Blend together and enjoy!

MIKE'S GREEN POWER DRINK

A great pre and post workout snack!

(V, G, H, A) | SERVES 1-2

Ingredients

large handful kale

large handful baby spinach

1 cup broccoli

2 carrots

1 apple

1 cup water (or 1/2 cup almond milk & 1/2 cup water)

1/2 cup ice

1 Tbsp. ground flaxseed

1 Tbsp. hemp oil

1 tsp. agave

Directions

Blend together and enjoy!

TOMATO FLAX SMOOTHIE

(V, G, H, A) | SERVES 1-2

Ingredients

2 cups tomatoes

1/2 apple

1 carrot

1 celery stalk

Tabasco or hot sauce, to taste

2 cups ice

1 Tbsp. ground flaxseed

1 Tbsp. hemp oil

Directions

Blend together and enjoy!

SUNRISE ORANGE SMOOTHIE

(V, G, H, A) | SERVES 1-2

Ingredients

2 oranges peeled

1 banana

1/2 cup strawberries

4 oz. plain Greek yogurt

1 cup ice

1 Tbsp. ground flaxseed

1 Tbsp. hemp oil

Directions

Blend together and enjoy!

CITRUS SMOOTHIE

(G, H, A) | SERVES 1-2

Ingredients

2 oranges

4 clementines

1 cup fresh pineapples

1 banana

1 cup almond milk or 4 oz. plain Greek yogurt

1 cup ice

1 Tbsp. ground flaxseed

1 Tbsp. hemp oil

Directions

Blend together and enjoy!

BANANA ALMOND BUTTER SMOOTHIE

(V, G, H, A) | SERVES 1-2

Ingredients

1 banana

1/2 cup strawberries

1/2 cup plain Greek yogurt or almond milk

2 Tbsp. carob nibs

1/4 cup almond butter

1 cup ice

1 Tbsp. ground flaxseed

2 Tbsp. water

Directions

Blend together and enjoy!

APPLE KALE SMOOTHIE

(V, G, H, A) | SERVES 1

Ingredients

- **1 apple**
- **1 carrot**
- **small handful kale**
- **1 cup water**
- **1/2 cup ice**
- **1 Tbsp. ground flaxseed**
- **1 Tbsp. hemp oil**
- **1 tsp. agave**

Directions

Blend together and enjoy!

GREEN STRAWBERRY SMOOTHIE

(V, G, H, A) | SERVES 1

Ingredients

2 cups strawberries

1/4 cup blueberries

1 head of broccoli

1 carrot

1 cup water

1/2 cup ice

1 Tbsp. ground flaxseed

1 Tbsp. hemp oil

1 tsp. agave

Directions

Blend together and enjoy!

MELON, DATE & KALE SMOOTHIE

(V, G, H, A) | SERVES 1

Ingredients

2 cups honeydew melon

handful kale

2 dates

1 cup water

1/2 cup ice

1 Tbsp. ground flaxseed

1 Tbsp. hemp oil

1 tsp. agave

Directions

Blend together and enjoy!

MORE RESOURCES

TWITTER
Follow Mike Dolce on Twitter @TheDolceDiet and read his "favorited tweets" for inspirational testimonials!

FACEBOOK
Check out The Dolce Diet fan page at Facebook.com/TheDolceDiet

YOUTUBE
Be sure to check out The Dolce Diet YouTube channel at YouTube.com/dolcediet for videos detailing exercises, recipes and so much more!

THE DOLCE DIET SOCIAL NETWORK
It's FREE! Design your own profile page at MYDolceDiet.com and talk with Mike during his frequent LIVE CHATS, as well as with others living healthy, vibrant lifestyles just like you!

THE DOLCE DIET OFFICIAL WEBSITE
Get the latest news about Mike, his athletes, health tips and more at TheDolceDiet.com

BOOKS BY MIKE DOLCE
#1 Bestseller The Dolce Diet: LIVING LEAN available at Amazon.com

The Dolce Diet: 3 WEEKS TO SHREDDED available at TheDolceDiet.com

For more information about Mike Dolce & The Dolce Diet visit TheDolceDiet.com

CPSIA information can be obtained at www.ICGtesting.com
Printed in the USA
LVOW011910200313

325138LV00014BA/41/P